ggplot2 Essentials

Explore the full range of ggplot2 plotting capabilities to create meaningful and spectacular graphs

Donato Teutonico

BIRMINGHAM - MUMBAI

ggplot2 Essentials

First published: June 2015

Production reference: 1220615

Published by Packt Publishing Ltd.
Livery Place
35 Livery Street
Birmingham B3 2PB, UK.

ISBN 978-1-78528-352-9

www.packtpub.com

Credits

Author
Donato Teutonico

Reviewers
Juanjo Abellan
Niels W. Hanson
Sefa Kilic

Commissioning Editor
Julian Ursell

Acquisition Editors
Tushar Gupta
Owen Roberts

Content Development Editor
Samantha Gonsalves

Technical Editor
Siddhesh Patil

Copy Editor
Sarang Chari

Project Coordinator
Kinjal Bari

Proofreader
Safis Editing

Indexer
Monica Mehta

Graphics
Disha Haria
Jason Monteiro

Production Coordinator
Arvindkumar Gupta

Cover Work
Arvindkumar Gupta

About the Author

Donato Teutonico has received his PharmD degree from the University of Turin, Italy, where he specialized in chemical and pharmaceutical technology, and his PhD in pharmaceutical sciences from Paris-South University, France. He has several years of experience in the modeling and simulation of drug effects and clinical trials in industrial and academic settings. Donato has contributed to numerous scientific projects and publications in international journals. In his work, he has been extensively using R for modeling, data analysis, and data visualization.

He is the author of two R packages for pharmacometrics—cts-template and panels-for-pharmacometrics—both of which are available on Google Code. He has also been a reviewer for Packt Publishing and is the author of *Instant R Starter*, *Packt Publishing*.

I would like to thank my beautiful wife, Raquel, and my son, Leonardo, for all their help and their joyful support in my private and professional life.

About the Reviewers

Juanjo Abellan is a mathematician and statistician by training. He has more than 20 years of experience as an applied statistician. He has held positions in public offices, academia, and industry in Spain, the UK, and Germany. He has authored and coauthored more than 30 articles that have been published in scientific journals. His current main interests include the application of Bayesian statistics in drug development, statistical methods for handling missing data in longitudinal clinical trials, and adaptive designs. He has been using R intensively since the late 1990s.

Niels W. Hanson has a BSc in computer science and a PhD in bioinformatics from the University of British Columbia, where he currently studies metagenomics and microbial ecology in the Steven J. Hallam Laboratory. He has had much experience in the analysis of large genomic datasets from human, aquatic, and terrestrial environments and has extensively utilized the R environment and ggplot2 in his research. His other research interests include software development, machine learning, data visualization, data mining, parallel algorithms, and distributed computing. Dr. Hanson is a reviewer of Institute of Electrical and Electronics Engineers (IEEE) journals and was an editorial reviewer of Tamara Munzner's *Visualization Analysis and Design*, a recent textbook on information visualization. He currently resides in Vancouver, British Columbia, where his hobbies include badminton, tennis, and downhill skiing.

Sefa Kilic is a PhD candidate in computational biology at the Department of Biological Sciences, University of Maryland, Baltimore County. He received his bachelor's and master's degrees in computer science from Middle East Technical University, Turkey.

For his graduate studies, he used machine learning, statistics, and information theory methods on large genomic data to understand how bacteria regulate the expression of their genes. He has years of experience in scientific computing and data visualization libraries in the Python and R ecosystems. He is also interested in functional programming.

www.PacktPub.com

Support files, eBooks, discount offers, and more

For support files and downloads related to your book, please visit www.PacktPub.com.

Did you know that Packt offers eBook versions of every book published, with PDF and ePub files available? You can upgrade to the eBook version at www.PacktPub.com and as a print book customer, you are entitled to a discount on the eBook copy. Get in touch with us at service@packtpub.com for more details.

At www.PacktPub.com, you can also read a collection of free technical articles, sign up for a range of free newsletters and receive exclusive discounts and offers on Packt books and eBooks.

https://www2.packtpub.com/books/subscription/packtlib

Do you need instant solutions to your IT questions? PacktLib is Packt's online digital book library. Here, you can search, access, and read Packt's entire library of books.

Why subscribe?

- Fully searchable across every book published by Packt
- Copy and paste, print, and bookmark content
- On demand and accessible via a web browser

Free access for Packt account holders

If you have an account with Packt at www.PacktPub.com, you can use this to access PacktLib today and view 9 entirely free books. Simply use your login credentials for immediate access.

Table of Contents

Preface

As a very powerful open source language, R is rapidly becoming a standard in the scientific community, particularly for data analysis and data visualization. This is related mainly to the vast availability of library packages, which empower the user to apply this software in virtually any field of scientific research. In relation to data visualization, R provides a rich palette of tools, and among the packages available, ggplot2 is fast becoming one of the more sophisticated and advanced packages. Its use is constantly growing in the community of R users. This increasing interest is particularly related to the ggplot2 capability of creating high-quality plots with a very appealing layout and coding that is sufficiently easy to use.

As a scripting language, R may be difficult to master, but in this book, you will find a large number of examples and tips as well as detailed explanations, which will provide you with all the necessary tools to understand the concepts behind ggplot2 in depth and concretely apply them to solve everyday problems related to data visualization. You will see step-by-step descriptions, ranging from the basic applications of ggplot2 in realizing simple plots up to the realization of more advanced and sophisticated plots. We will also dig into controlling plot details, which will enable you to perform a full customization of the plot you intend to realize. Finally, we will also see more special applications of ggplot2, for instance, regarding how to include map data in plots, realize heatmaps, and realize matrix scatterplots using additional packages based on ggplot2.

By the end of this book, you will not only have learned how to use the full potential of ggplot2, but you will also be able to generate publication-quality plots. Moreover, you will also be able to use this book and its examples as a reference for daily questions concerning the use of ggplot2 for data representation.

What this book covers

Chapter 1, Graphics in R, gets you up and running with R and ggplot2 by providing you with a description of the R installation as well as the integrated development environment you may want to use in your daily use of R. You will also be introduced to the general ideas behind the different packages available for data visualization, graphics and lattice, and you will also see a few examples of how different plots realized with these packages can be realized with ggplot2. This will provide you with a quick reference to the similarities and differences among the different versions of code if you are already familiar with the other packages.

Chapter 2, Getting Started, provides you with an easy start to ggplot2 and the different plots that can be realized. We will see different plot examples using the qplot (quick plot) function, which provides you with a simplified tool to easily generate plots. In this chapter, we will go through histograms, density plots, bar charts, boxplots, scatterplots, time series, and dot charts.

Chapter 3, The Layers and Grammar of Graphics, gives you a general introduction to the different components on which the grammar of graphics is based. Such components are, for instance, the scales, coordinate system, faceting, aesthetic, and geometry. Understanding these is crucial for the use of the full potential of this package since only understanding the layered grammar can provide you with the right overview of how the different components are connected to each other. In this chapter, you will also find a series of tables summarizing the options available for function arguments, such as geometry and statistics, and they are intended to provide you with a reference for consultation when needed.

Chapter 4, Advanced Plotting Techniques, presents a few more advanced features and plots that can be realized in ggplot2. Building on the knowledge you will have developed, we will see how the grammar components can be combined to generate more complex plots. You will see how more advanced aesthetic mapping can be realized, for instance, using variables generated from statistical analysis or how components such as text and reference lines can be included on a plot. We will then also see how polar coordinate systems can be used to generate pie charts and other types of plots.

Chapter 5, Controlling Plot Details, shows you how you can modify the plot details as well as the default plot layout. You will see how we can modify the plot title, axis, and legend appearance and position. Moreover, you will also see how themes can be used to completely customize the plot appearance without affecting the data represented.

Chapter 6, Plot Output, shows you how to modify and organize multiple plots after their realization. We will see how to reproduce multiple plots next to each other and save the plots in different file formats from the R console, as well as using scripting commands.

Chapter 7, Special Applications of ggplot2, shows you examples of the special application of ggplot2 and other packages based on ggplot2. We will see how we can include maps in plots as well as add data to such maps; we will see how we can draw scatterplot matrices to represent the relationships between different variables. Finally, we will see how we can realize heat maps.

What you need for this book

To get the most out of this book, you will need to install R on your computer, as well as the ggplot2 package. Additional packages, such as ggmap and GGally, will also be used in *Chapter 7, Special Applications of ggplot2*. In *Chapter 1, Graphics in R*, you will find a detailed description of how you can install R and additional packages on your computer. You will also find additional information concerning additional programming interfaces such as RStudio.

Who this book is for

This book is perfect for R programmers who are interested in learning to use ggplot2 for a different type of data visualization—from the basics up to using more advanced applications, such as faceting and grouping. Since this book will not cover the basics of R commands and objects, you should have a basic understanding of the R language.

Conventions

In this book, you will find a number of text styles that distinguish between different kinds of information. Here are some examples of these styles and an explanation of their meaning.

Code words in text, database table names, folder names, filenames, file extensions, pathnames, dummy URLs, user input, and Twitter handles are shown as follows: " The qplot (quick plot) function is a basic high-level function of ggplot2"

Any command-line input or output is written as follows:

```
plot(age~circumference, data=Orange)
```

New terms and **important words** are shown in bold. Words that you see on the screen, for example, in menus or dialog boxes, appear in the text like this: "For instance, the **Animation** and **Documentary** types have a much smaller sample size compared with the other categories"

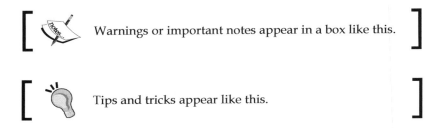

Warnings or important notes appear in a box like this.

Tips and tricks appear like this.

Reader feedback

Feedback from our readers is always welcome. Let us know what you think about this book—what you liked or disliked. Reader feedback is important for us as it helps us develop titles that you will really get the most out of.

To send us general feedback, simply e-mail feedback@packtpub.com, and mention the book's title in the subject of your message.

If there is a topic that you have expertise in and you are interested in either writing or contributing to a book, see our author guide at www.packtpub.com/authors.

Customer support

Now that you are the proud owner of a Packt book, we have a number of things to help you to get the most from your purchase.

Downloading the example code

You can download the example code files from your account at http://www.packtpub.com for all the Packt Publishing books you have purchased. If you purchased this book elsewhere, you can visit http://www.packtpub.com/support and register to have the files e-mailed directly to you.

Downloading the color images of this book

We also provide you with a PDF file that has color images of the screenshots/ diagrams used in this book. The color images will help you better understand the changes in the output. You can download this file from `http://www.packtpub.com/ sites/default/files/downloads/35290S_ColoredImages.pdf`.

Errata

Although we have taken every care to ensure the accuracy of our content, mistakes do happen. If you find a mistake in one of our books—maybe a mistake in the text or the code—we would be grateful if you could report this to us. By doing so, you can save other readers from frustration and help us improve subsequent versions of this book. If you find any errata, please report them by visiting `http://www.packtpub. com/submit-errata`, selecting your book, clicking on the **Errata Submission Form** link, and entering the details of your errata. Once your errata are verified, your submission will be accepted and the errata will be uploaded to our website or added to any list of existing errata under the Errata section of that title.

To view the previously submitted errata, go to `https://www.packtpub.com/books/ content/support` and enter the name of the book in the search field. The required information will appear under the **Errata** section.

Piracy

Piracy of copyrighted material on the Internet is an ongoing problem across all media. At Packt, we take the protection of our copyright and licenses very seriously. If you come across any illegal copies of our works in any form on the Internet, please provide us with the location address or website name immediately so that we can pursue a remedy.

Please contact us at `copyright@packtpub.com` with a link to the suspected pirated material.

We appreciate your help in protecting our authors and our ability to bring you valuable content.

Questions

If you have a problem with any aspect of this book, you can contact us at `questions@packtpub.com`, and we will do our best to address the problem.

1
Graphics in R

The objective of this chapter is to provide you with a general overview of the plotting environments in R and of the most efficient way of coding your graphs in it. We will go through the most important **Integrated Development Environment (IDE)** available for R as well as the most important packages available for plotting data; this will help you to get an overview of what is available in R and how those packages are compared with ggplot2. Finally, we will dig deeper into the grammar of graphics, which represents the basic concepts on which ggplot2 was designed. But first, let's make sure that you have a working version of R on your computer.

Getting ggplot2 up and running

If you have this book in your hands, it is very likely you already have a working version of R installed on your computer. If this is not the case, you can download the most up-to-date version of R from the R project website (http://www.r-project.org/). There, you will find a direct connection to the **Comprehensive R Archive Network (CRAN)**, a network of FTP and web servers around the world that store identical, up-to-date versions of code and documentation for R. In addition to access to the CRAN servers, on the website of the R project, you may also find information about R, a few technical manuals, the R journal, and details about the packages developed for R and stored in the CRAN repositories.

At the time of writing, the current version of R is 3.1.2. If you have already installed R on your computer, you can check the actual version with the R.Version() code, or for a more concise result, you can use the R.version.string code that recalls only part of the output of the previous function.

Packages in R

In the next few pages of this chapter, we will quickly go through the most important visualization packages available in R, so in order to try the code, you will also need to have additional packages as well as `ggplot2` up and running in your R installation. In the basic R installation, you will already have the `graphics` package available and loaded in the session; the `lattice` package is already available among the standard packages delivered with the basic installation, but it is not loaded by default. `ggplot2`, on the other hand, will need to be installed. You can install and load a package with the following code:

```
> install.packages("ggplot2")
> library(ggplot2)
```

Keep in mind that every time R is started, you will need to load the package you need with the `library(name_of_the_package)` command to be able to use the functions contained in the package. In order to get a list of all the packages installed on your computer, you can use the call to the `library()` function without arguments. If, on the other hand, you would like to have a list of the packages currently loaded in the workspace, you can use the `search()` command. One more function that can turn out to be useful when managing your library of packages is `.libPaths()`, which provides you with the location of your R libraries. This function is very useful to trace back the package libraries you are currently using, if any, in addition to the standard library of packages, which on Windows is located by default in a path of the kind `C:/Program Files/R/R-3.1.2/library`.

The following list is a short recap of the functions just discussed:

```
.libPaths()   # get library location
library()     # see all the packages installed
search()      # see the packages currently loaded
```

The Integrated Development Environment

You will definitely be able to run the code and the examples shown in this book directly from the standard R **Graphical User Interface (GUI)**, especially if you are frequently working with R in more complex projects or simply if you like to keep an eye on the different components of your code, such as scripts, plots, and help pages, you may well think about the possibility of using an IDE. The number of specific IDEs that get integrated with R is still limited, but some of them are quite efficient, well-designed and open source.

RStudio

RStudio (`http://www.rstudio.com/`) is a very nice and advanced programming environment developed specifically for R, and this would be my recommended choice of IDE as the R programming environment in most cases. It is available for all the major platforms (Windows, Linux, and Mac OS X), and it can be run on a local machine, such as your computer, or even over the Web, using **RStudio Server**. With RStudio Server, you can connect a browser-based interface (the RStudio IDE) to a version of R running on a remote Linux server.

RStudio allows you to integrate several useful functionalities, in particular if you use R for a more complex project. The way the software interface is organized allows you to keep an eye on the different activities you very often deal with in R, such as working on different scripts, overviewing the installed packages, as well as having easy access to the help pages and the plots generated. This last feature is particularly interesting for `ggplot2` since in RStudio, you will be able to easily access the history of the plots created instead of visualizing only the last created plot, as is the case in the default R GUI. One other very useful feature of RStudio is code completion. You can, in fact, start typing a comment, and upon pressing the *Tab* key, the interface will provide you with functions matching what you have written . This feature will turn out to be very useful in `ggplot2`, so you will not necessarily need to remember all the functions and you will also have guidance for the arguments of the functions as well.

In *Figure 1.1*, you can see a screenshot from the current version of RStudio (v 0.98.1091):

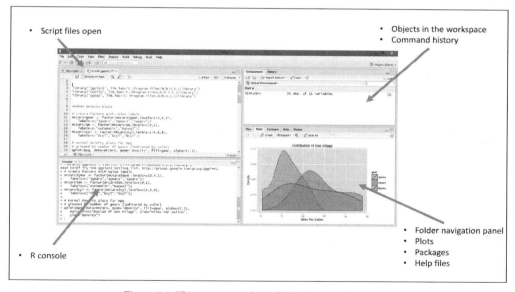

Figure 1.1: This is a screenshot of RStudio on Windows 8

The environment is composed of four different areas:

- **Scripting area**: In this area you can open, create, and write the scripts.
- **Console area**: This area is the actual R console in which the commands are executed. It is possible to type commands directly here in the console or write them in a script and then run them on the console (I would recommend the last option).
- **Workspace/History area**: In this area, you can find a practical summary of all the objects created in the workspace in which you are working and the history of the typed commands.
- **Visualization area**: Here, you can easily load packages, open R help files, and, even more importantly, visualize plots.

The RStudio website provides a lot of material on how to use the program, such as manuals, tutorials, and videos, so if you are interested, refer to the website for more details.

Eclipse and StatET

Eclipse (http://www.eclipse.org/) is a very powerful IDE that was mainly developed in Java and initially intended for Java programming. Subsequently, several extension packages were also developed to optimize the programming environment for other programming languages, such as C++ and Python. Thanks to its original objective of being a tool for advanced programming, this IDE is particularly intended to deal with very complex programming projects, for instance, if you are working on a big project folder with many different scripts. In these circumstances, Eclipse could help you to keep your programming scripts in order and have easy access to them. One drawback of such a development environment is probably its big size (around 200 MB) and a slightly slow-starting environment.

Eclipse does not support interaction with R natively, so in order to be able to write your code and execute it directly in the R console, you need to add **StatET** to your basic Eclipse installation. StatET (http://www.walware.de/goto/statet) is a plugin for the Eclipse IDE, and it offers a set of tools for R coding and package building. More detailed information on how to install Eclipse and StatET and how to configure the connections between R and Eclipse/StatET can be found on the websites of the related projects.

Emacs and ESS

Emacs (http://www.gnu.org/software/emacs/) is a customizable text editor and is very popular, particularly in the Linux environment. Although this text editor appears with a very simple GUI, it is an extremely powerful environment, particularly thanks to the numerous keyboard shortcuts that allow interaction with the environment in a very efficient manner after getting some practice. Also, if the user interface of a typical IDE, such as RStudio, is more sophisticated and advanced, Emacs may be useful if you need to work with R on systems with a poor graphical interface, such as servers and terminal windows. Like Eclipse, Emacs does not support interfacing with R by default, so you will need to install an add-on package on your Emacs that will enable such a connection, **Emacs Speaks Statistics (ESS)**. ESS (http://ess.r-project.org/) is designed to support the editing of scripts and interacting with various statistical analysis programs including R. The objective of the ESS project is to provide efficient text editor support to statistical software, which in some cases comes with a more or less defined GUI, but for which the real power of the language is only accessible through the original scripting language.

The plotting environments in R

R provides a complete series of options to realize graphics, which makes it quite advanced with regard to data visualization. Along the next few sections of this chapter, we will go through the most important R packages for data visualization by quickly discussing some high-level differences and analogies. If you already have some experience with other R packages for data visualization, in particular `graphics` or `lattice`, the following sections will provide you with some references and examples of how the code used in such packages appears in comparison with that used in `ggplot2`. Moreover, you will also have an idea of the typical layout of the plots created with a certain package, so you will be able to identify the tool used to realize the plots you will come across.

The core of graphics visualization in R is within the `grDevices` package, which provides the basic structure of data plotting, such as the colors and fonts used in the plots. Such a graphic engine was then used as the starting point in the development of more advanced and sophisticated packages for data visualization, the most commonly used being `graphics` and `grid`.

The `graphics` package is often referred to as the base or traditional graphics environment since, historically, it was the first package for data visualization available in R, and it provides functions that allow the generation of complete plots.

The `grid` package, on the other hand, provides an alternative set of graphics tools. This package does not directly provide functions that generate complete plots, so it is not frequently used directly to generate graphics, but it is used in the development of advanced data visualization packages. Among the grid-based packages, the most widely used are `lattice` and `ggplot2`, although they are built by implementing different visualization approaches — `Trellis` plots in the case of `lattice` and the grammar of graphics in the case of `ggplot2`. We will describe these principles in more detail in the coming sections. A diagram representing the connections between the tools just mentioned is shown in *Figure 1.2*. Just keep in mind that this is not a complete overview of the packages available but simply a small snapshot of the packages we will discuss. Many other packages are built on top of the tools just mentioned, but in the following sections, we will focus on the most relevant packages used in data visualization, namely `graphics`, `lattice`, and, of course, `ggplot2`. If you would like to get a more complete overview of the graphics tools available in R, you can have a look at the web page of the R project summarizing such tools, `http://cran.r-project.org/web/views/Graphics.html`.

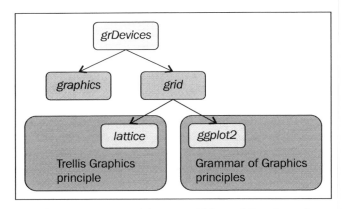

Figure 1.2: This is an overview of the most widely used R packages for graphics

In order to see some examples of plots in `graphics`, `lattice` and `ggplot2`, we will go through a few examples of different plots over the following pages. The objective of providing these examples is not to do an exhaustive comparison of the three packages but simply to provide you with a simple comparison of how the different codes as well as the default plot layouts appear for these different plotting tools. For these examples, we will use the `Orange` dataset available in R; to load it in the workspace, simply write the following code:

```
>data(Orange)
```

This dataset contains records of the growth of orange trees. You can have a look at the data by recalling its first lines with the following code:

```
>head(Orange)
```

You will see that the dataset contains three columns. The first one, `Tree`, is an ID number indicating the tree on which the measurement was taken, while `age` and `circumference` refer to the age in days and the size of the tree in millimeters, respectively. If you want to have more information about this data, you can have a look at the help page of the dataset by typing the following code:

```
?Orange
```

Here, you will find the reference of the data as well as a more detailed description of the variables included.

Standard graphics and grid-based graphics

The existence of these two different graphics environments brings these questions to most users' minds—which package to use and under which circumstances? For simple and basic plots, where the data simply needs to be represented in a standard plot type (such as a scatter plot, histogram, or boxplot) without any additional manipulation, then all the plotting environments are fairly equivalent. In fact, it would probably be possible to produce the same type of plot with `graphics` as well as with `lattice` or `ggplot2`. Nevertheless, in general, the default graphic output of `ggplot2` or `lattice` will be most likely superior compared to `graphics` since both these packages are designed considering the principles of human perception deeply and to make the evaluation of data contained in plots easier.

When more complex data should be analyzed, then the grid-based packages, `lattice` and `ggplot2`, present a more sophisticated support in the analysis of multivariate data. On the other hand, these tools require greater effort to become proficient because of their flexibility and advanced functionalities. In both cases, `lattice` and `ggplot2`, the package provides a full set of tools for data visualization, so you will not need to use `grid` directly in most cases, but you will be able to do all your work directly with one of those packages.

Graphics and standard plots

The `graphics` package was originally developed based on the experience of the graphics environment in R. The approach implemented in this package is based on the principle of the pen-on-paper model, where the plot is drawn in the first function call and once content is added, it cannot be deleted or modified.

In general, the functions available in this package can be divided into high-level and low-level functions. High-level functions are functions capable of drawing the actual plot, while low-level functions are functions used to add content to a graph that was already created with a high-level function.

Downloading the example code

You can download the example code files from your account at http://www.packtpub.com for all the Packt Publishing books you have purchased. If you purchased this book elsewhere, you can visit http://www.packtpub.com/support and register to have the files e-mailed directly to you.

Let's assume that we would like to have a look at how age is related to the circumference of the trees in our dataset `Orange`; we could simply plot the data on a scatter plot using the high-level function `plot()` as shown in the following code:

```
plot(age~circumference, data=Orange)
```

This code creates the graph in *Figure 1.3*. As you would have noticed, we obtained the graph directly with a call to a function that contains the variables to plot in the form of $y\sim x$, and the dataset to locate them. As an alternative, instead of using a formula expression, you can use a direct reference to x and y, using code in the form of `plot(x,y)`. In this case, you will have to use a direct reference to the data instead of using the data argument of the function. Type in the following code:

```
plot(Orange$circumference, Orange$age)
```

The preceding code results in the following output:

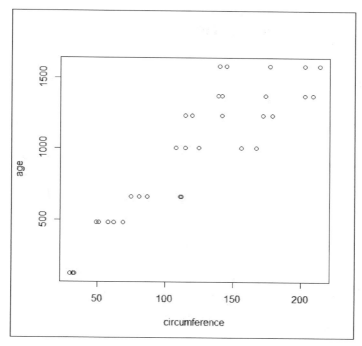

Figure 1.3: Simple scatterplot of the dataset Orange using graphics

For the time being, we are not interested in the plot's details, such as the title or the axis, but we will simply focus on how to add elements to the plot we just created. For instance, if we want to include a regression line as well as a smooth line to have an idea of the relation between the data, we should use a low-level function to add the just-created additional lines to the plot; this is done with the `lines()` function:

```
plot(age~circumference, data=Orange)    ###Create basic plot
abline(lm(Orange$age~Orange$circumference), col="blue")
lines(loess.smooth(Orange$circumference,Orange$age), col="red")
```

The graph generated as the output of this code is shown in *Figure 1.4*:

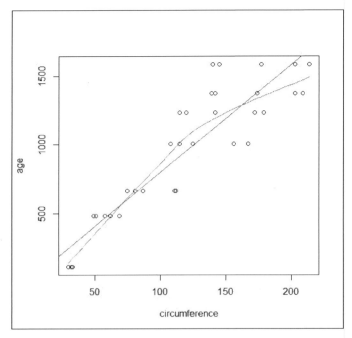

Figure 1.4: This is a scatterplot of the Orange data with a regression line
(in blue) and a smooth line (in red) realized with graphics

As illustrated, with this package, we have built a graph by first calling one function, which draws the main plot frame, and then additional elements were included using other functions. With graphics, only additional elements can be included in the graph without changing the overall plot frame defined by the `plot()` function. This ability to add several graphical elements together to create a complex plot is one of the fundamental elements of R, and you will notice how all the different graphical packages rely on this principle. If you are interested in getting other code examples of plots in graphics, there is also some demo code available in R for this package, and it can be visualized with `demo(graphics)`.

In the coming sections, you will find a quick reference to how you can generate a similar plot using `graphics` and `ggplot2`. As will be described in more detail later on, in `ggplot2`, there are two main functions to realize plots, `ggplot()` and `qplot()`. The function `qplot()` is a wrapper function that is designed to easily create basic plots with `ggplot2`, and it has a similar code to the `plot()` function of `graphics`. Due to its simplicity, this function is the easiest way to start working with `ggplot2`, so we will use this function in the examples in the following sections. The code in these sections also uses our example dataset `Orange`; in this way, you can run the code directly on your console and see the resulting output.

Scatterplots with individual data points

To generate the plot generated using `graphics`, use the following code:

```
plot(age~circumference, data=Orange)
```

The preceding code results in the following output:

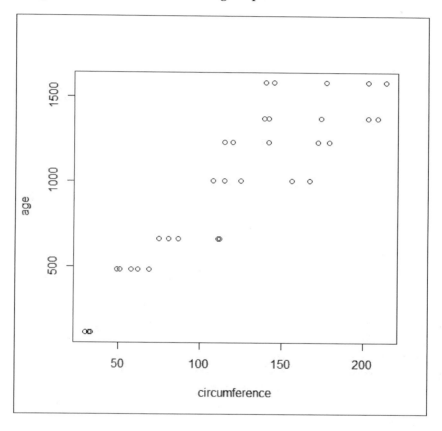

To generate the plot using `ggplot2`, use the following code:

```
qplot(circumference,age, data=Orange)
```

The preceding code results in the following output:

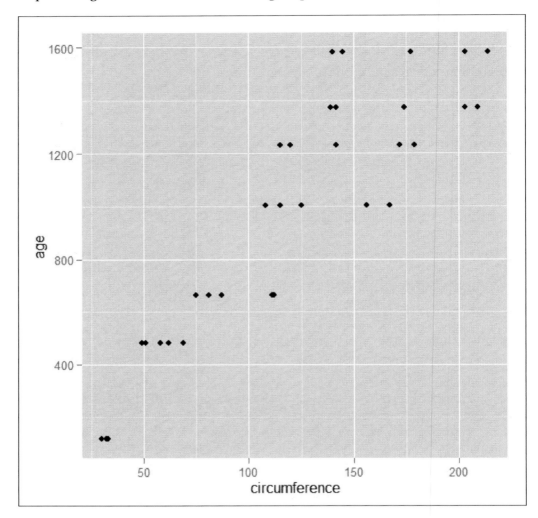

Scatterplots with the line of one tree

To generate the plot using `graphics`, use the following code:

```
plot(age~circumference, data=Orange[Orange$Tree==1,], type="l")
```

The preceding code results in the following output:

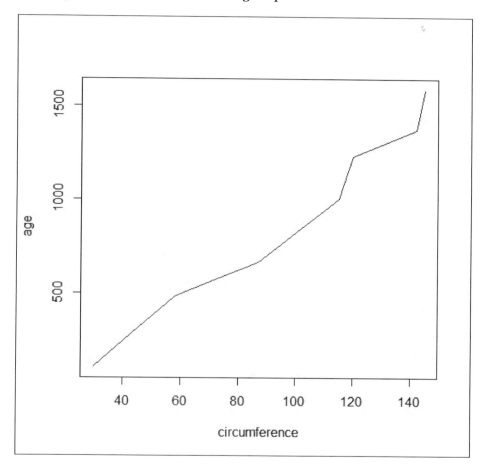

To generate the plot using `ggplot2`, use the following code:

```
qplot(circumference,age, data=Orange[Orange$Tree==1,],
geom="line")
```

The preceding code results in the following output:

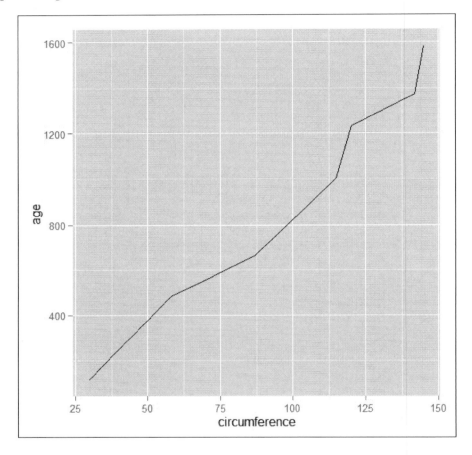

Scatterplots with the line and points of one tree

To generate the plot using `graphics`, use the following code:

```
plot(age~circumference, data=Orange[Orange$Tree==1,], type="b")
```

The preceding code results in the following output:

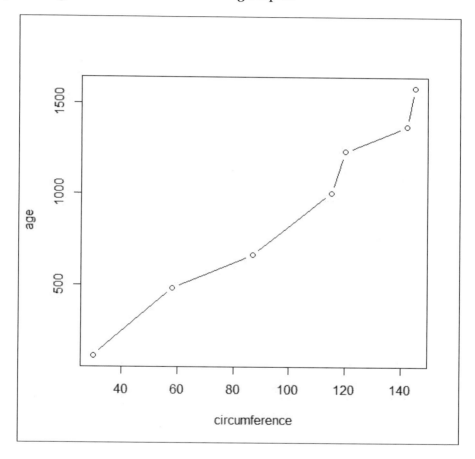

To generate the plot using ggplot2, use the following code:

```
qplot(circumference,age, data=Orange[Orange$Tree==1,],
geom=c("line","point"))
```

The preceding code results in the following output:

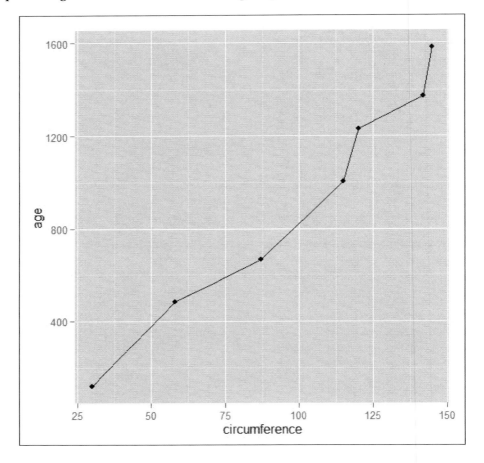

Boxplots of the orange dataset

To generate the plot using `graphics`, use the following code:

```
boxplot(circumference~Tree, data=Orange)
```

The preceding code results in the following output:

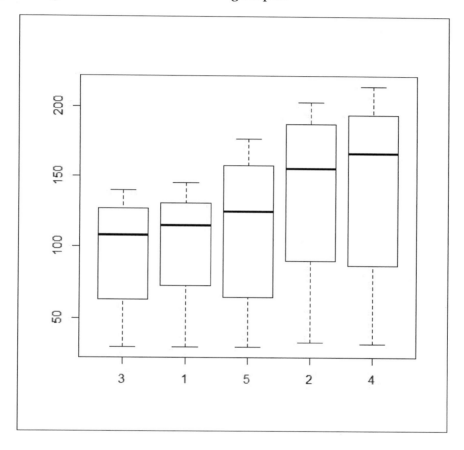

To generate the plot using `ggplot2`, use the following code:

```
qplot(Tree,circumference, data=Orange, geom="boxplot")
```

The preceding code results in the following output:

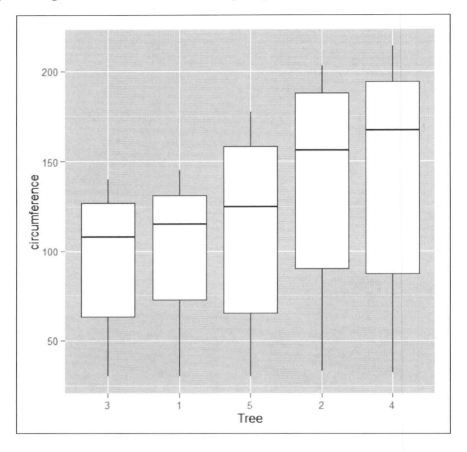

Boxplots with individual observations

To generate the plot using `graphics`, use the following code:

```
boxplot(circumference~Tree, data=Orange)
points(circumference~Tree, data=Orange)
```

The preceding code results in the following output:

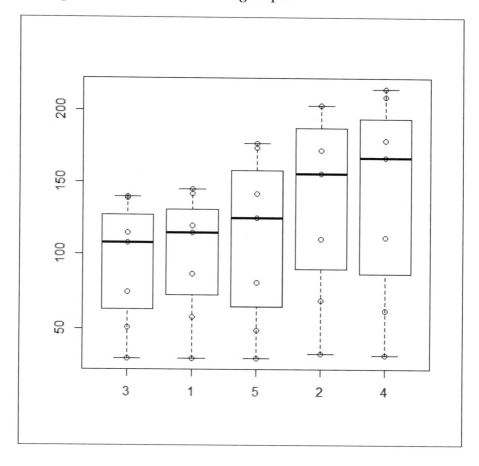

To generate the plot using `ggplot2`, use the following code:

```
qplot(Tree,circumference, data=Orange, geom=c("boxplot","point"))
```

The preceding code results in the following output:

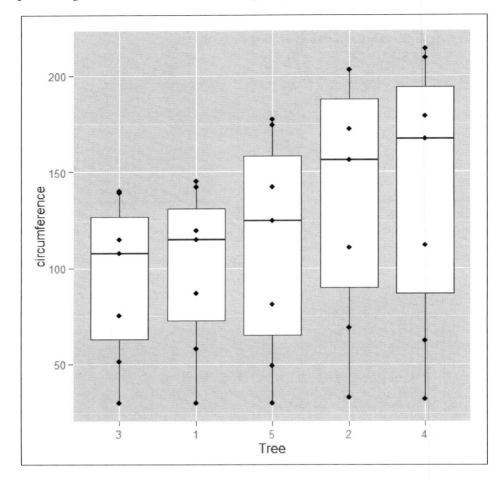

Histograms of the orange dataset

To generate the plot using `graphics`, use the following code:

```
hist(Orange$circumference)
```

The preceding code results in the following output:

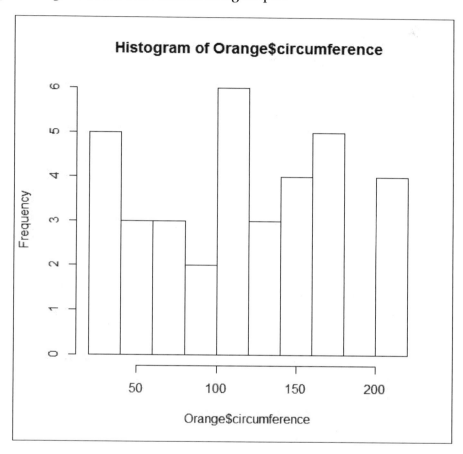

To generate the plot using `ggplot2`, use the following code:

```
qplot(circumference, data=Orange, geom="histogram")
```

The preceding code results in the following output:

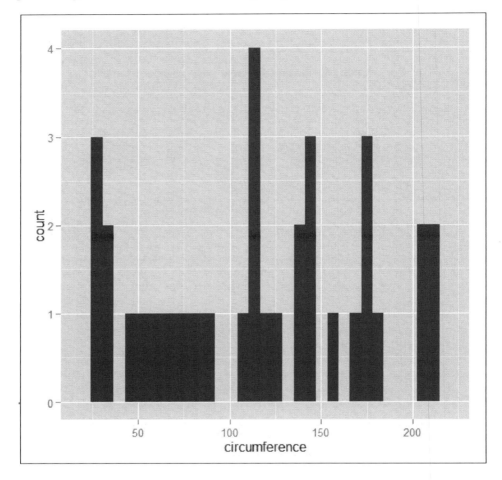

Histograms with the reference line at the median value in red

To generate the plot using `graphics`, use the following code:

```
hist(Orange$circumference)
abline(v=median(Orange$circumference), col="red")
```

The preceding code results in the following output:

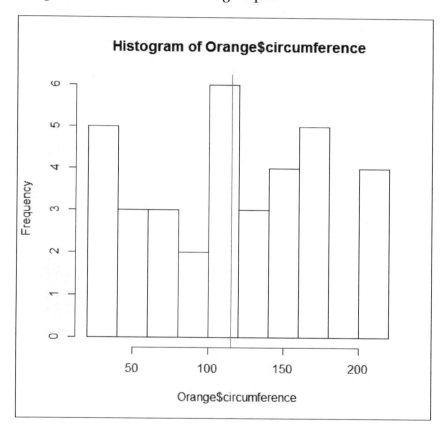

To generate the plot using ggplot2, use the following code:

```
qplot(circumference, data=Orange,
geom="histogram")+geom_vline(xintercept =
median(Orange$circumference),
colour="red")
```

The preceding code results in the following output:

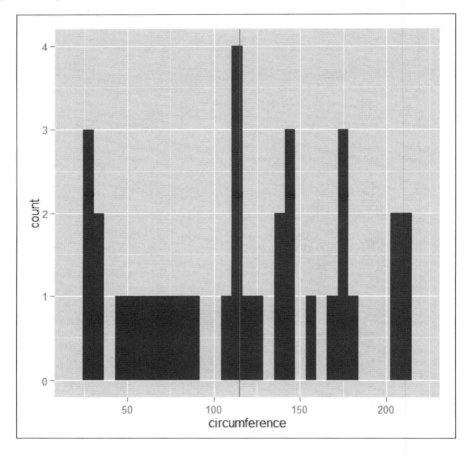

Lattice and Trellis plots

Along with with `graphics`, the base R installation also includes the `lattice` package. This package implements a family of techniques known as Trellis graphics, proposed by William Cleveland to visualize complex datasets with multiple variables. The objective of those design principles was to ensure the accurate and faithful communication of data information. These principles are embedded into the package and are already evident in the default plot design settings. One interesting feature of Trellis plots is the option of *multipanel conditioning*, which creates multiple plots by splitting the data on the basis of one variable. A similar option is also available in `ggplot2`, but in that case, it is called *faceting*.

In `lattice`, we also have functions that are able to generate a plot with one single call, but once the plot is drawn, it is already final. Consequently, plot details as well as additional elements that need to be included in the graph, need to be specified already within the call to the main function. This is done by including all the specifications in the panel function argument. These specifications can be included directly in the main body of the function or specified in an independent function, which is then called; this last option usually generates more readable code, so this will be the approach used in the following examples. For instance, if we want to draw the same plot we just generated in the previous section with graphics, containing the age and circumference of trees and also the regression and smooth lines, we need to specify such elements within the function call. You may see an example of the code here; remember that `lattice` needs to be loaded in the workspace:

```
require(lattice)              ##Load lattice if needed
myPanel <- function(x,y){
panel.xyplot(x,y)             # Add the observations
panel.lmline(x,y,col="blue")  # Add the regression
panel.loess(x,y,col="red")    # Add the smooth line
}
xyplot(age~circumference, data=Orange, panel=myPanel)
```

This code produces the plot in *Figure 1.5*:

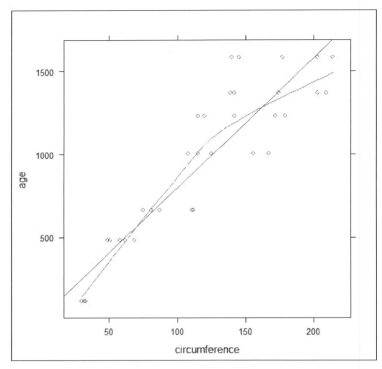

Figure 1.5: This is a scatter plot of the Orange data with the regression line (in blue) and
the smooth line (in red) realized with lattice

As you would have noticed, taking aside the code differences, the plot generated
does not look very different from the one obtained with graphics. This is because
we are not using any special visualization feature of lattice. As mentioned earlier,
with this package, we have the option of multipanel conditioning, so let's take a look
at this. Let's assume that we want to have the same plot but for the different trees in
the dataset. Of course, in this case, you would not need the regression or the smooth
line, since there will only be one tree in each plot window, but it could be nice to
have the different observations connected. This is shown in the following code:

```
myPanel <- function(x,y){
panel.xyplot(x,y, type="b") #the observations
}
xyplot(age~circumference | Tree, data=Orange, panel=myPanel)
```

This code generates the graph shown in *Figure 1.6*:

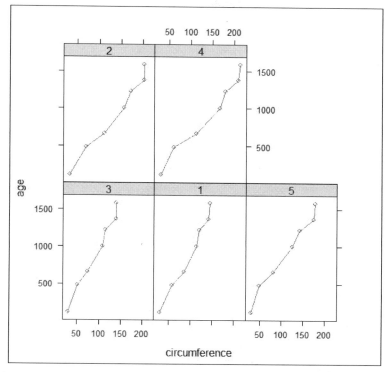

Figure 1.6: This is a scatterplot of the Orange data realized with lattice, with one subpanel representing the individual data of each tree. The number of trees in each panel is reported in the upper part of the plot area

As illustrated, using the vertical bar |, we are able to obtain the plot conditional to the value of the variable `Tree`. In the upper part of the panels, you would notice the reference to the value of the conditional variable, which, in this case, is the column `Tree`. As mentioned before, `ggplot2` offers this option too; we will see one example of that in the next section.

In the next section, You would find a quick reference to how to convert a typical plot type from `lattice` to `ggplot2`. In this case, the examples are adapted to the typical plotting style of the `lattice` plots.

Scatterplots with individual observations

To plot the graph using `lattice`, use the following code:

```
xyplot(age~circumference, data=Orange)
```

The preceding code results in the following output:

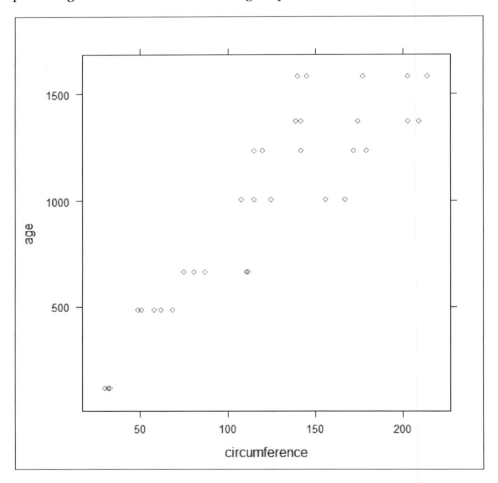

To plot the graph using ggplot2, use the following code:

```
qplot(circumference,age, data=Orange)
```

The preceding code results in the following output:

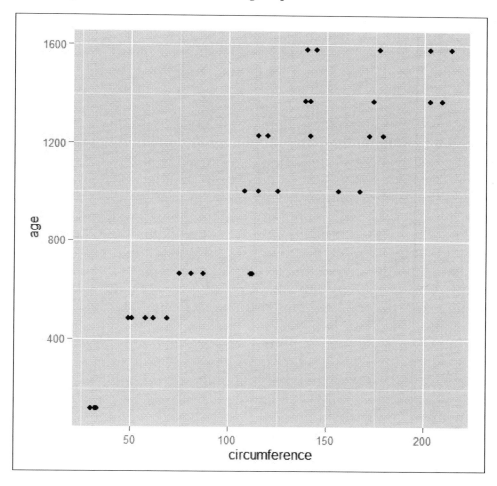

Scatterplots of the orange dataset with faceting

To plot the graph using `lattice`, use the following code:

```
xyplot(age~circumference|Tree, data=Orange)
```

The preceding code results in the following output:

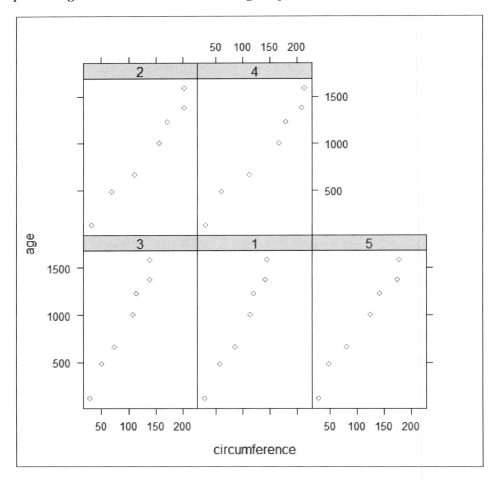

To plot the graph using `ggplot2`, use the following code:

```
qplot(circumference,age, data=Orange, facets=~Tree)
```

The preceding code results in the following output:

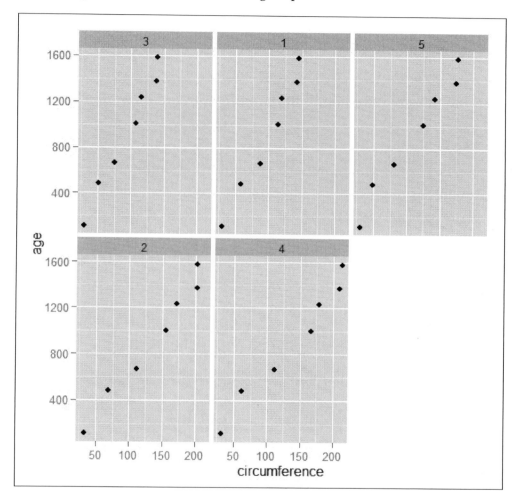

Faceting scatterplots with line and points

To plot the graph using `lattice`, use the following code:

```
xyplot(age~circumference|Tree, data=Orange, type="b")
```

The preceding code results in the following output:

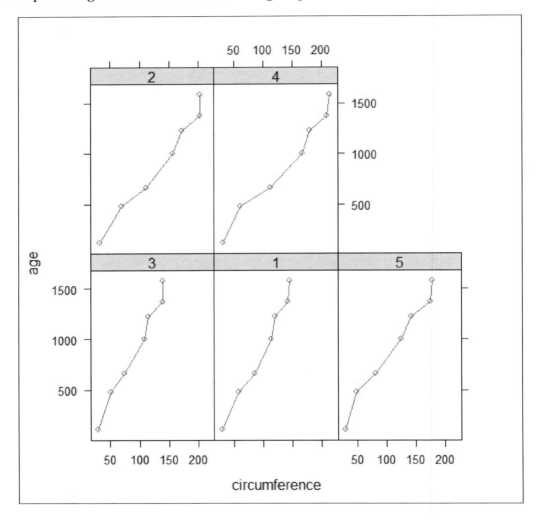

To plot the graph using `ggplot2`, use the following code:

```
qplot(circumference,age, data=Orange, geom=c("line","point"),
facets=~Tree)
```

The preceding code results in the following output:

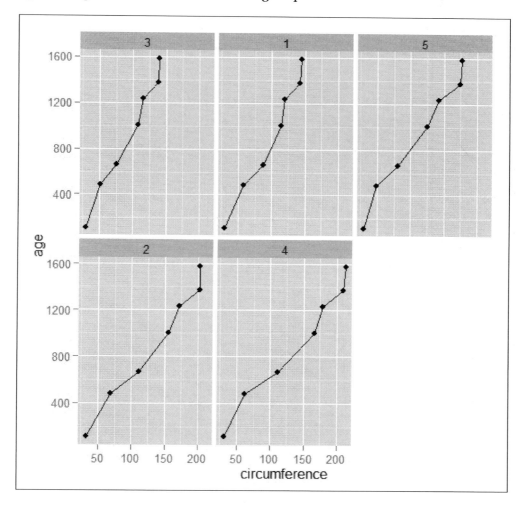

Scatterplots with grouping data

To plot the graph using `lattice`, use the following code:

```
xyplot(age~circumference, data=Orange, groups=Tree, type="b")
```

The preceding code results in the following output:

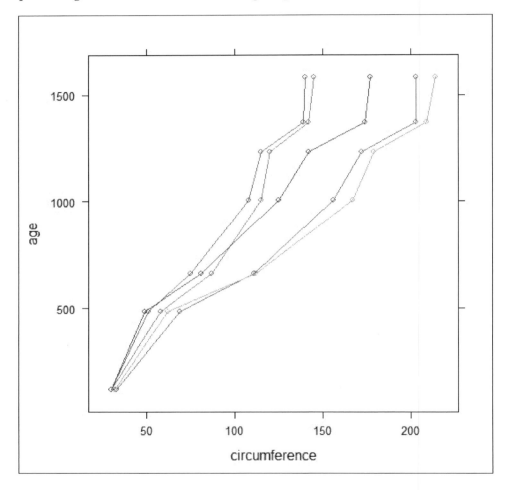

To plot the graph using `ggplot2`, use the following code:

```
qplot(circumference,age, data=Orange,color=Tree,
geom=c("line","point"))
```

The preceding code results in the following output:

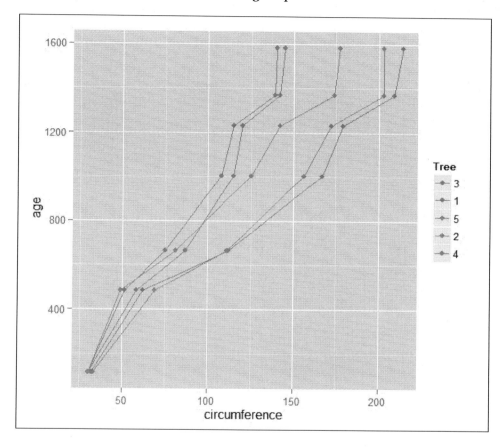

Boxplots of the orange dataset

To plot the graph using `lattice`, use the following code:

```
bwplot(circumference~Tree, data=Orange)
```

The preceding code results in the following output:

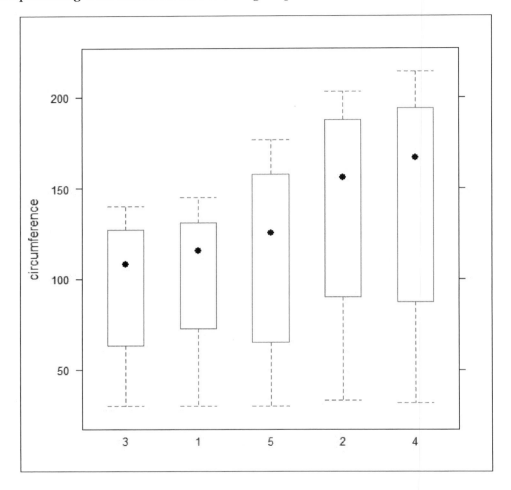

To plot the graph using `ggplot2`, use the following code:

```
qplot(Tree,circumference, data=Orange, geom="boxplot")
```

The preceding code results in the following output:

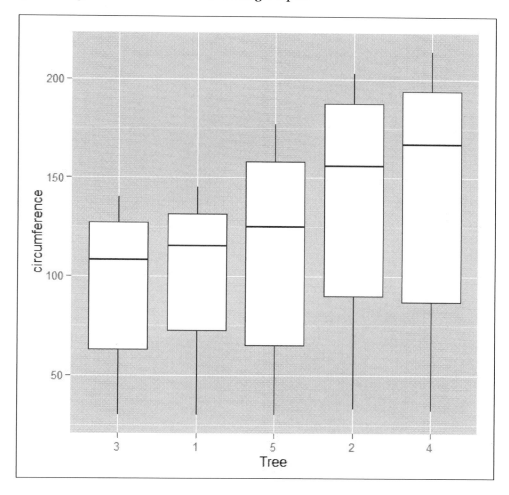

Histograms of the orange dataset

To plot the graph using `lattice`, use the following code:

```
histogram(Orange$circumference, type = "count")
```

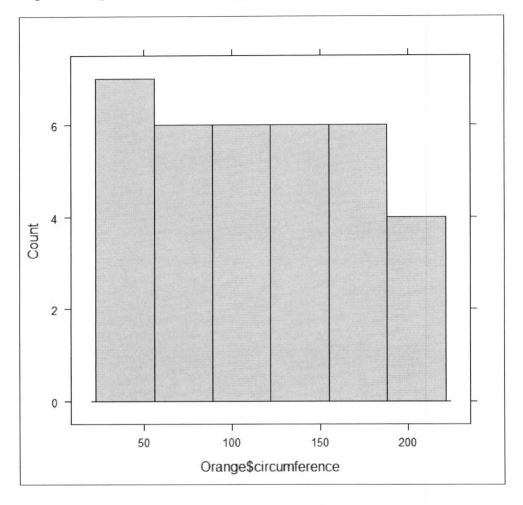

To plot the graph using `ggplot2`, use the following code:

```
qplot(circumference, data=Orange, geom="histogram")
```

The preceding code results in the following output:

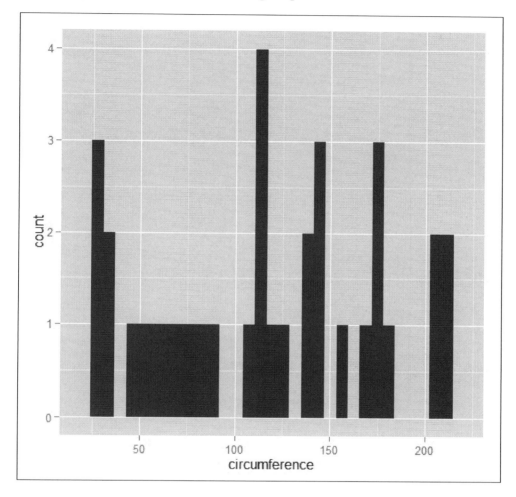

Histograms with the reference line at the median value in red

To plot the graph using `lattice`, use the following code:

```
histogram(~circumference, data=Orange, type = "count",
panel=function(x,...){panel.histogram(x,
...);panel.abline(v=median(x), col="red")})
```

The preceding code results in the following output:

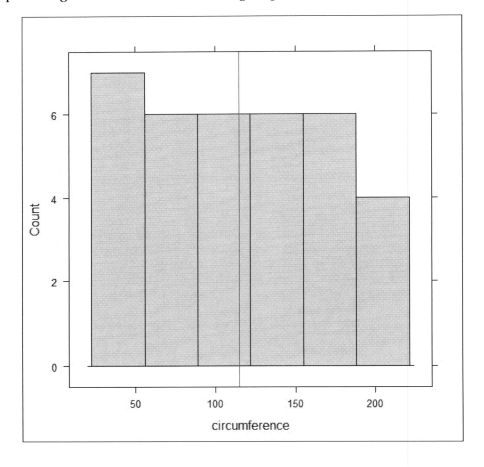

To plot the graph using `ggplot2`, use the following code:

```
qplot(circumference, data=Orange,
geom="histogram")+geom_vline(xintercept =
median(Orange$circumference),
colour="red")
```

The preceding code results in the following output:

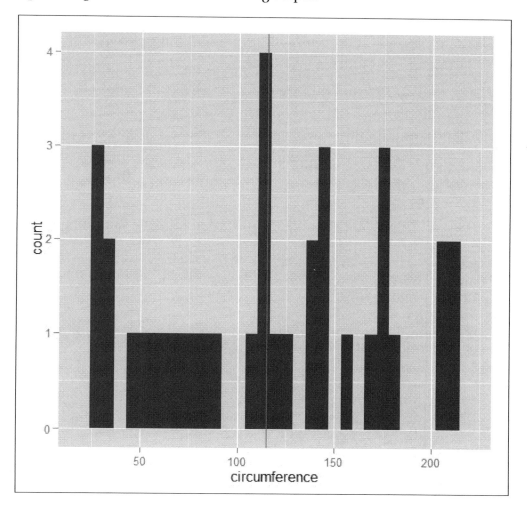

ggplot2 and the grammar of graphics

The `ggplot2` package was developed by Hadley Wickham by implementing a completely different approach to statistical plots. As is the case with `lattice`, this package is also based on `grid`, providing a series of high-level functions that allow the creation of complete plots. The `ggplot2` package provides an interpretation and extension of the principles of the book *The Grammar of Graphics* by *Leland Wilkinson*. Briefly, *The Grammar of Graphics* assumes that a statistical graphic is a mapping of data to the aesthetic attributes and geometric objects used to represent data, such as points, lines, bars, and so on. Besides the aesthetic attributes, the plot can also contain statistical transformation or grouping of data. As in `lattice`, in `ggplot2`, we have the possibility of splitting data by a certain variable, obtaining a representation of each subset of data in an independent subplot; such representation in `ggplot2` is called faceting.

In a more formal way, the main components of the grammar of graphics are the data and its mapping, aesthetics, geometric objects, statistical transformations, scales, coordinates, and faceting. We will cover each one of these elements in more detail in *Chapter 3*, *The Layers and Grammar of Graphics*, but for now, consider these general principles:

- The data that must be visualized is mapped to **aesthetic attributes**, which define how the data should be perceived
- **Geometric objects** describe what is actually displayed on the plot, such as lines, points, or bars; the geometric objects basically define which kind of plot you are going to draw
- **Statistical transformations** are applied to the data to group them; examples of statistical transformations would be the smooth line or the regression lines of the previous examples or the binning of the histograms
- **Scales** represent the connection between the aesthetic spaces and the actual values that should be represented. Scales may also be used to draw legends
- **Coordinates** represent the coordinate system in which the data is drawn
- **Faceting**, which we have already mentioned, is the grouping of data in subsets defined by a value of one variable

In `ggplot2`, there are two main high-level functions capable of directly creating a plot, `qplot()`, and `ggplot()`; `qplot()` stands for quick plot, and it is a simple function that serves a purpose similar to that served by the `plot()` function in `graphics`. The `ggplot()` function, on the other hand, is a much more advanced function that allows the user to have more control of the plot layout and details. In our journey into the world of `ggplot2`, we will see some examples of `qplot()`, in particular when we go through the different kinds of graphs, but we will dig a lot deeper into `ggplot()` since this last function is more suited to advanced examples.

If you have a look at the different forums based on R programming, there is quite a bit of discussion as to which of these two functions would be more convenient to use. My general recommendation would be that it depends on the type of graph you are drawing more frequently. For simple and standard plots, where only the data should be represented and only the minor modification of standard layouts are required, the `qplot()` function will do the job. On the other hand, if you need to apply particular transformations to the data or if you would just like to keep the freedom of controlling and defining the different details of the plot layout, I would recommend that you focus on `ggplot()`. As you will see, the code between these functions is not completely different since they are both based on the same underlying philosophy, but the way in which the options are set is quite different, so if you want to adapt a plot from one function to the other, you will essentially need to rewrite your code. If you just want to focus on learning only one of them, I would definitely recommend that you learn `ggplot()`.

In the following code, you will see an example of a plot realized with `ggplot2`, where you can identify some of the components of the grammar of graphics. The example is realized with the `ggplot()` function, which allows a more direct comparison with the grammar of graphics, but coming just after the following code, you could also find the corresponding `qplot()` code useful. Both codes generate the graph depicted in *Figure 1.7*:

```
require(ggplot2)                          ## Load ggplot2
data(Orange)                              ## Load the data


ggplot(data=Orange,                       ## Data used
   aes(x=circumference,y=age, color=Tree))+   ## Aesthetic
geom_point()+                             ## Geometry
stat_smooth(method="lm",se=FALSE)         ## Statistics


### Corresponding code with qplot()
qplot(circumference,age,data=Orange,      ## Data used
   color=Tree,                            ## Aesthetic mapping
   geom=c("point","smooth"),method="lm",se=FALSE)
```

This simple example can give you an idea of the role of each portion of code in a ggplot2 graph; you have seen how the main function body creates the connection between the data and the aesthetics we are interested to represent and how, on top of this, you add the components of the plot, as in this case, we added the geometry element of points and the statistical element of regression. You can also notice how the components that need to be added to the main function call are included using the + sign. One more thing worth mentioning at this point is that if you run just the main body function in the ggplot() function, you will get an error message. This is because this call is not able to generate an actual plot. The step during which the plot is actually created is when you include the geometric attribute, which, in this case is geom_point(). This is perfectly in line with the grammar of graphics since, as we have seen, the geometry represents the actual connection between the data and what is represented on the plot. This is the stage where we specify that the data should be represented as points; before that, nothing was specified about which plot we were interested in drawing.

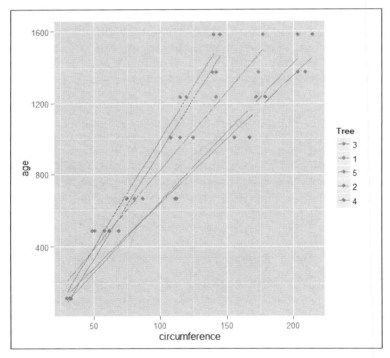

Figure 1.7: This is an example of plotting the Orange dataset with ggplot2

Further reading

- *R Graphics (2nd edition), P. Murrell, CRC Press*
- *The Grammar of Graphics (Statistics and Computing) (2nd edition), L. Wilkinson, Springer*
- *Lattice: Multivariate Data Visualization with R (Use R!), D. Sarkar, Springer*
- *S-PLUS Trellis Graphics User's Manual, R. Becker and W. Cleveland, MathSoft Inc*

Summary

In this chapter, we set up your installation of R and made sure that you are ready to start creating the `ggplot2` plots. You saw the different packages available to realize plots in R and their history and relations. The `graphics` package is the first package that was developed in R; it represents a simple and effective tool to realize plots. Subsequently, the `grid` package was introduced with more advanced control of the plot elements as well as more advanced graphics functionalities. Several packages were then built on top of `grid`, in particular `lattice` and `ggplot2`, providing high-level functions for advanced data representation. In the next chapter, we will explore some important plot types that can be realized with `ggplot2`. You will also be introduced to faceting.

2
Getting Started

In this chapter, we will go through the main plot types that can be realized with ggplot2. In the examples, we will use the qplot() basic function so that you have a reference for how to realize such plots, even if you are not interested in a more detailed personalization of the graph details. We will see how to realize the following plots:

- Histograms and density plots
- Bar charts
- Boxplots
- Scatterplots
- Time series plots
- Bubble charts and dot plots

In *Chapter 3*, *The Layers and Grammar of Graphics*, we will describe the use of the ggplot function, and in the equivalent coding between qplot and ggplot, we will also discuss how to realize the plots with such a sophisticated function.

General aspects

The qplot (quick plot) function is a basic high-level function of ggplot2. The general syntax that you should use with this function is the following:

```
qplot(x, y, data, color, shape, size, facets, geom, stat)
```

The definitions of the various components of this function are as follows:

- x and y: These represent the variables to plot (y is optional, with a default value of NULL).
- data: This defines the dataset containing the variables.

- `color`, `shape` and `size`: These are the aesthetic arguments that can be mapped on additional variables.

- `facets`: This defines the optional faceting of the plot based on one variable contained in the dataset.

- `geom`: This allows you to select the actual visualization of the data, which, basically, will define the plot that will be generated. The possible values are `point`, `line`, and `boxplot`, and we will see several different examples in the next pages.

- `stat`: This defines the statistics to be used for the data.

These arguments represent the most important options available in `qplot()`. You can find descriptions of the other arguments of this function on the help page of the function, accessible with `?qplot` or on the `ggplot2` website at `http://docs.ggplot2.org/0.9.3/qplot.html`.

Thanks to the way the grammar of graphics was conceived, most of the previously mentioned arguments can be applied to different types of plots. For instance, you can use the color argument to do an aesthetics mapping to one variable, and you can do that on a scatter plot as well as a histogram. Exactly the same concept can be seen in facets, which you can use to split data into subplots, independently of the type of plot considered.

Before moving on to the different plots, we should clarify some details about the syntax of aesthetic mapping and faceting, so that you are able to adapt the coming examples to different situations.

Introduction to aesthetic attributes

In `ggplot2`, the `color`, `shape`, and `size` of graphical objects are aesthetic attributes that are usually mapped to the value of a variable contained in the data. For instance, in your dataset, if you have different series of measurements, you can associate the color attribute with a flag variable and have each series of data in a different color, exactly as we did in *Chapter 1, Graphics in R* in section *ggplot2 and the grammar of graphics*, with the following code:

```
qplot(circumference,age,data=Orange, color=Tree,
geom=c("point","smooth"),method="lm", se=FALSE)
```

This generates a plot (see *Figure 1.7*) where each series of data from the same tree will have the same color and its relative regression line. We will go into more details on this point in *Chapter 3, The Layers and Grammar of Graphics*, but for now, what is important to know is that if you want to have, for instance, all the data with the same color, you will need to use the `I()` function. So, in order to get the same plot with all the data in blue, you will need to specify `color=I("blue")`.

Exactly the same principle applies to `size` and `shape` attributes, which you can map to a variable or specify using `I()`, where, for instance, `size=I(3)` would produce bigger symbols and `shape=I(2)` would produce triangles instead of dots.

Introduction to faceting

You can use faceting to create multiple plots by creating a subplot for each level of a categorical variable. The general code for faceting would be `facets=a~b`, where a and b represent two categorical variables for which data is split. This code would generate a grid containing a subplot for each combination of the a and b variables. However, quite often you may be interested in faceting only relative to one variable; in this case, you would use a code such as `facets=a~.`, where the period indicates that there is no second faceting variable.

How to change the faceting orientation

When using faceting, you may need to change the panel orientation. This is done by changing the order of the variables, so `facets=a~b` create one row for each value of a and one column for each value of b, while b~a will do it the other way around. Just remember that the same applies when you only have one variable. So `facets=a~.` will create one row for each value of a, while `facets=.~a` will arrange the plots in columns.

Histograms and density plots

Histograms are plots used to explore how one or more quantitative variables are distributed. To show some examples of histograms, we will use the *iris* data. This dataset contains measurements in centimetres of the length and width variables of the sepal and petal, and these measurements are available for 50 flowers from each of three species of iris: *Iris setosa*, *versicolor*, and *virginica*. You can get more details upon running `?iris`.

The geometric attribute used to produce histograms is defined simply by specifying `geom="histogram"` in the `qplot` function. This default histogram will represent the variable specified in the function on the *x* axis, while the *y* axis will represent the number of elements in each bin. One other very useful way of representing distributions is to look at the kernel density function, which represents an approximation of the distribution of the data as a continuous function instead of different bins, by estimating the probability density function.

For example, let's plot the petal length of all three species of `iris` as a histogram and as a density plot with the following code:

```
qplot(Petal.Length, data=iris, geom="histogram")    ## Histogram
qplot(Petal.Length, data=iris, geom="density")       ## Density plot
```

The output of this code is showed in *Figure 2.1*:

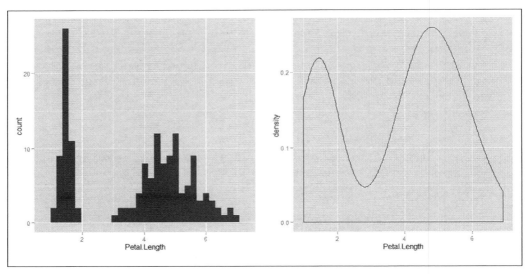

Figure 2.1: This shows a histogram (left) and a density plot (right)

As you can see in both plots of *Figure 2.1*, it appears that the data is not distributed uniformly, but there are at least two distinct distributions clearly separated. This is due to a different distribution for one of the `iris` species. To verify that the two distributions are indeed related to species differences, we could generate the same plot using aesthetic attributes and have a different color for each subtype of `iris`. To do this, we can simply map color to the `Species` column in the dataset; in this case we can also do that for both the histogram and the density plot. This is shown in the following code:

```
qplot(Petal.Length, data=iris, geom="histogram", color=Species)
qplot(Petal.Length, data=iris, geom="density", color=Species)
```

Figure 2.2 is the result of the preceding code:

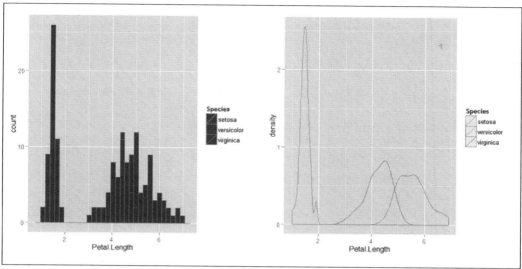

Figure 2.2: Histogram (left) and density plot (right) with aesthetic attribute for color

As you have seen in *Figure 2.2*, mapping a categorical variable to an aesthetic attribute has automatically split geom of the plot by that variable. In the distributions represented in our plots, the lower petal lengths are shown coming from the **setosa** species, while the two other distributions are partly overlapping. This clarifies our question about the distribution of the data, but the plots we have obtained are not really nice, since the color in this case has affected only the borders of the plot elements. In fact, in ggplot2, we have access to the fill argument defining, as you can easily imagine, the filling of the graphical elements. So, let's color the inside of the histogram and the density plot; we are interested in having the inside the same color as the border, so we can also map the fill argument to the Species variable, as we already did for the color argument. The following is the code we built:

```
qplot(Petal.Length, data=iris, geom="histogram", color=Species,
fill=Species)
```

```
qplot(Petal.Length, data=iris, geom="density", color=Species,
fill=Species)
```

Figure 2.3 shows the resulting output:

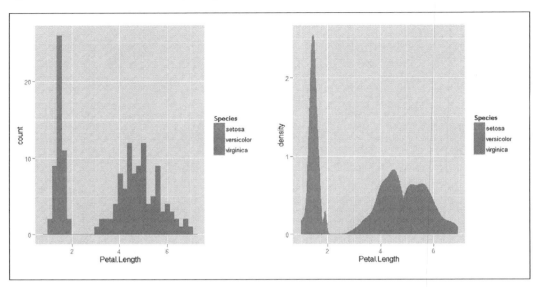

Figure 2.3: This shows the histogram (left) and the density plot (right) with aesthetic attributes for color and fill

As illustrated, the plot we now have is definitely better than the previous one. On the other hand, there is still an improvement that we could make to the graphical visualization of the data. The plot now has quite strong colors, so we could add some transparency to make the plot elements much nicer. In ggplot2, this is done with the alpha argument. This argument can be used to make colors transparent by selecting the degree of transparency between 0 (completely transparent) and 1 (completely opaque). There are many possible applications of this argument, but for the time being, we will use the basic assignment in qplot(). Just remember that since this is an aesthetic parameter, you need to use the I() function, since we are not mapping something, but simply assigning a value of transparency. So in our case, this would be our code:

```
qplot(Petal.Length, data=iris, geom="histogram", color=Species,
fill=Species, alpha=I(0.5))
```

```
qplot(Petal.Length, data=iris, geom="density", color=Species,
fill=Species, alpha=I(0.5))
```

In *Figure 2.4*, we have the resulting plots, and now the result is quite nice:

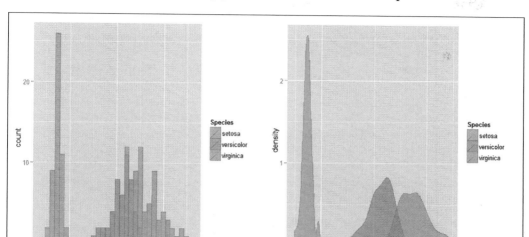

Figure 2.4: This shows the histogram (left) and the density plot (right) with aesthetic attributes for color and fill plus transparency with alpha included

After running the code provided in the previous examples, you would have probably noticed the warning message on the console informing the user that the program is choosing the size of the bins used in the histogram. As an alternative, the bin size can also be also specified in the `qplot` function using the `binwidth` argument, which controls the smoothing level of the histogram by setting the bin size. Evaluating different bin sizes can be very important, since it can greatly affect the visualization of your data.

Bar charts

Bar charts are usually used to explore how one (or more) categorical variables are distributed. In `qplot()`, this is done using the `geom` option *bar*. This geometry counts the number of occurrences of each factor variable, which appears in the data. To show an example of the bar chart, we will use the `movies` dataset, which is included within the `ggplot2` package. We have already seen how to recall the dataset included with the basic installation of R, but if you are interested in the list of datasets within a specific package (`ggplot2` in this case), you can use the following code:

```
require(ggplot2)        ## Load ggplot2 if needed
data(package="ggplot2")  ## List of dataset within ggplot2
```

The `movies` dataset contains information about movies, including the rating, from the `http://imdb.com/` website. You can get a more detailed description in the help page of the dataset.

This dataset contains different variables but, for our example, we will not need all of them, so let's rearrange a bit of its content. For our exercise, we are first interested in knowing how many movies were produced in each category - *Action, Animation, Comedy, Drama, Documentary,* and *Romance*. Let's also keep in the dataset the information about the movie budget, whether it was a short or regular movie, its year, and so on. So, the steps covered in our code are:

1. Load the data.
2. Extract from the dataset the information for each movie type concerning budget and length.
3. Create a factor variable containing the movie type.

The header of our final dataset, called `myMovieData`, will then be `Budget`, `Short`, `Year`, and `Type`. So, here's our code:

```
d1 <-data.frame(movies[movies$Action==1, c("budget", "Short",
"year")])

d1$Type <- "Animation"

d2 <-data.frame(movies[movies$Animation==1, c("budget", "Short",
"year")])

d2$Type <- "Animation"

d3 <-data.frame(movies[movies$Comedy==1, c("budget", "Short",
"year")])

d3$Type <- "Comedy"

d4 <-data.frame(movies[movies$Drama==1, c("budget", "Short",
"year")])

d4$Type <- "Drama"

d5 <-data.frame(movies[movies$Documentary==1, c("budget", "Short",
"year")])

d5$Type <- "Documentary"

d6 <-data.frame(movies[movies$Romance==1, c("budget", "Short",
"year")])

d6$Type <- "Romance"

myMovieData <- rbind(d1, d2, d3, d4, d5, d6)

names(myMovieData) <- c("Budget", "Short", "Year", "Type" )
```

Now that our data is ready, let's create our first bar chart. In general, we will follow the same structure as the other plots, just replacing the `geom` specification:

```
qplot(Type, data=myMovieData , geom="bar", fill=Type)
```

This standard bar chart will generate bars representing the count of each element (the movie type) for each type available. Since we have also assigned the `fill` aesthetic attribute to the same type variable, we also obtain the coloring of each bar in a different way. The plot generated is represented in *Figure 2.5*:

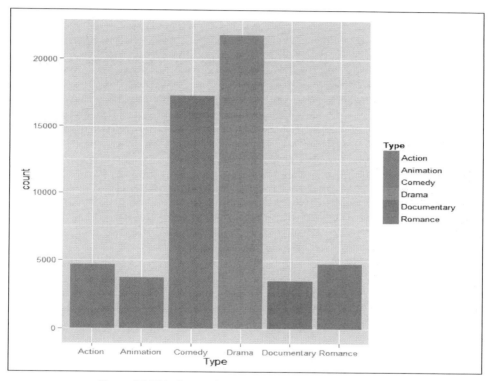

Figure 2.5: This shows a bar chart of the different movie types

In the plot we just created, the bars are colored differently depending on the movie type. However, we can use the `fill` argument in a more useful way. In fact, we could also require a different color based on the value of a second variable, in this way adding more information to the plot. In our simple example, we can split each bar by the relative amount of a short or regular movie. This is done simply by assigning the `Short` column to the `fill` argument as shown in the following code:

```
qplot(Type, data=myMovieData , geom="bar", fill=factor(Short))
```

The result is shown in *Figure 2.6*. As illustrated, we can now see the movie counts for short and regular movies, summing up the total number of movies for each type.

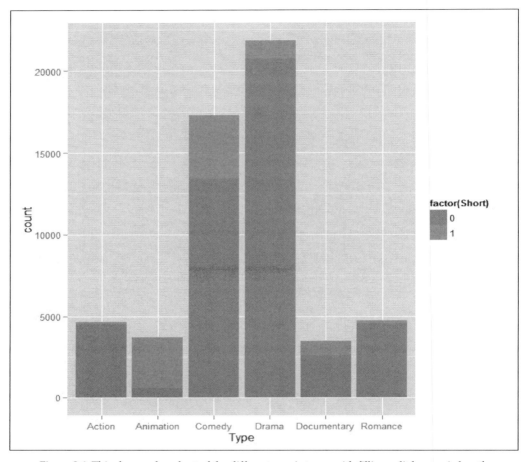

Figure 2.6: This shows a bar chart of the different movie types with filling split by movie length

As you probably noticed in this last example, we assigned the Short variable to the fill argument, but in the assignment, we also converted the variable to factor, while in the previous example, when we used the Type variable, we did not do so. The reason is that the fill aesthetic attribute, in this case, needed a discrete variable, which defined different levels. These, in turn, were assigned to different colors. The Type variable of the previous example was already a factor, where each level represented the movie type. On the other hand, the Short variable is actually numeric: 0 for regular movies and 1 for short movies. For this reason, we had to convert it first to a factor, so qplot could identify this variable as indicating two levels of a discrete variable. We will also discuss in detail the assignment of discrete and continuous variables in *Chapter 4, Advanced Plotting Techniques*. You can check out the class of the two columns with the following code:

```
> class(myMovieData$Short)
[1] "integer"
> class(myMovieData$Type)
[1] "factor"
```

One last thing to mention about bar charts is the position argument of the qplot function. Such argument defines the way you would like to display the bars within the chart. The three main options are stack, dodge, and fill. The stack option puts the bars with the same *x* value on top of each other; the dodge option places the bars next to each other for the same *x* value; and the fill option places the bars on top of each other but normalizes the height to 1. The following code shows the position adjustment applied to our last example:

```
qplot(Type, data=myMovieData, geom="bar", fill=factor(Short),
position="stack")

qplot(Type, data=myMovieData, geom="bar", fill=factor(Short),
position="dodge")

qplot(Type, data=myMovieData, geom="bar", fill=factor(Short),
position="fill")
```

Figure 2.7 shows you the resulting plot for each option:

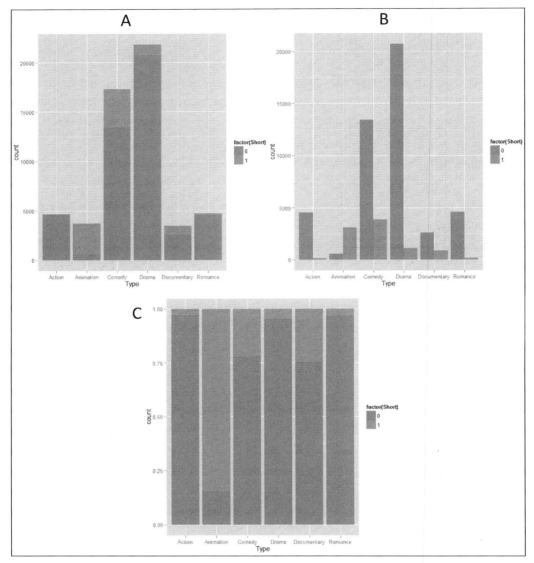

Figure 2.7: This shows the bar chart of different movie types with filling split by
movie length for different displays of bars—stack (A), dodge (B), and fill (C)

Boxplots

Box plots, also known as box-and-whisker plots, are a type of plot used to depict a distribution by representing its quartile values. In such plots, the upper and lower sides of the box represent the twenty-fifth and seventy-fifth percentiles (also called the first and third quartiles), while the horizontal line within the box represents the median of the data. The difference between the first and third quartiles is defined as **Inter-Quartile Range (IQR)**, and it is often used as a measure of statistical dispersion of a distribution. The upper whisker represents the higher values up to 1.5*IQR of the upper quartile, while the lower whisker represents lower values within 1.5*IQR of the lower quartile. The pieces of data not in the whisker range are plotted as points and are defined as *outliers*. You can get additional details and references in the package website shown at the end of the chapter.

In this section, we will see some examples of boxplots using the dataset created in the previous section, `myMovieData`, so please refer to previous examples of how to create such datasets. In this case, we will have a look at the budget of the movies present in the dataset. More precisely, we are interested in the budgets of different types of movies. In order to produce a boxplot, we will just need to specify a boxplot geometry. As illustrated in the next code, the command is exactly the same as the one used in the bar chart example; we have just chosen a different geometry to represent the data. The following code shows this:

```
qplot(Type,Budget, data=myMovieData, geom="boxplot")
```

The resulting plot is represented in *Figure 2.8*. You probably have seen a warning message appearing on the screen, such as the following:

Warning message:

Removed 49699 rows containing non-finite values (stat_boxplot).

This is simply because in the data, there are many NA values in the `column` budget, and the function informs us that these values were removed when representing the distribution.

Removing NA values

When working with data and distributions, you will probably come across the need to exclude NA values from your dataset. You can see an example of how such values could be excluded from the dataset of the previous example, that of `myMovieData`. The following code shows this:

```
myMovieData <- myMovieData [!is.na(myMovieData
$Budget),]
```

In the boxplot that we just produced, as outputted in *Figure 2.8*, we obtained the desired result - the distribution of budget values for the different categories of movies. You can clearly see the outlier values represented as points. Since the budget for the documentaries is very low compared to other movies, we cannot clearly see their values. In such cases, it may be useful to plot the log-transformed data so that, in the plots, the values are easier to compare visually. Of course, you will have to keep in mind that, in this case, the y axis will represent magnitudes in the log scale.

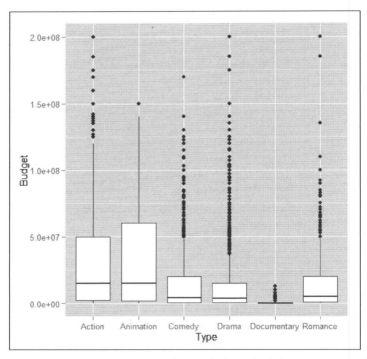

Figure 2.8: This shows a standard box plot of movie budgets for different categories of movies

One option to obtain the log transformation of the data can be to simply use the `log()` function when recalling the variable to transform and using the `log(Budget)` code. On the other hand, the more elegant way of plotting log-transformed values is via the `log` argument of the `qplot` function. Such an argument can have values of `"x"`, `"y"` or `"xy"`, which simply indicates which axis you are interested in having log-transformed — whether x, y or both. Just remember that the quotes should be also included in the code. With this option, the scale of the transformed axis is also changed in the log scale. With the alternative coding for direct data transformation, you have probably noted that both options produce the same plot — just with some differences in the y-scale notation. The following code shows this:

```
qplot(Type, Budget, data=myMovieData, geom="boxplot", log="y")
```

```
## Equivalent coding
qplot(Type, log(Budget), data=myMovieData, geom="boxplot")
```

The preceding code results in the following output:

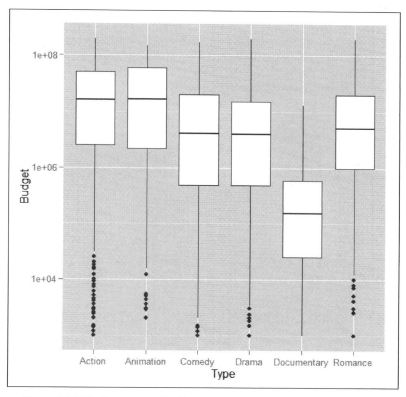

Figure 2.9: This shows a standard boxplot of movie budgets for the different
categories of movies with the y axis in the log scale

As illustrated in *Figure 2.9*, the resulting plot with the *y* axis in the log scale shows
the movie budgets better distributed in the central area of the plot, allowing a better
visual comparison of the data.

A very useful option in boxplots is the ability to visualize actual data points. This is
particularly useful since it allows you to see where the observed values are actually
located, with respect to the values of the descriptive statistics (median and quartiles).
In order to do that in ggplot2, we simply need to add the `"point"` geometry together
with the `"boxplot"` geometry. The following code shows this:

```
qplot(Type, Budget, data=myMovieData, geom=c("boxplot","point"),
log="y")
```

Bear in mind that `geom` attributes in `qplot` can be combined in vectors using `c()`. Combining these attributes will also give you the possibility of trying several combinations of attributes in order to create the plot you have in mind. Also, consider that the order of the elements in the vector will define the order of plotting. This means that in our case, with `geom=c("boxplot","point")`, we will have the points on top of the box plot. You can try to inverse the order and you will see how the points are covered by the boxplot.

The following graph is the output of the preceding code:

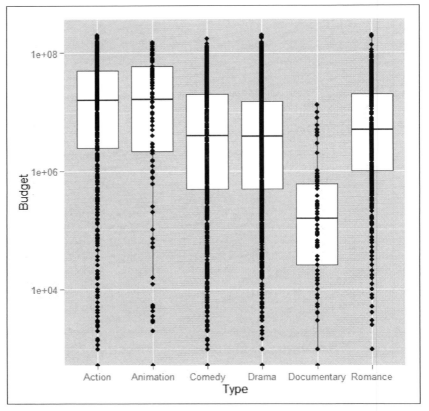

Figure 2.10: This shows a standard boxplot of movie budgets for different categories of movies, including data points (y axis in the log scale)

As you can see in *Figure 2.10*, we now have the data points included in our plot. Although data points in the boxplot are useful in some cases, in this example, this generates a sort of over-plotting, since we have too many data points and we end up with just a sort of vertical bar in the middle of our box plot. This is definitely not very helpful. Having data points a little separated from each other along the x axis could be a good way of improving our visualization. Luckily for us, in ggplot2, we have the option of jittering the data. Jittering is a process of adding random noise to data in order to prevent over-plotting in statistical graphs. As illustrated in the following code, it is done in quite a straightforward way by changing the geometry:

```
qplot(Type,Budget, data=myMovieData, geom=c("boxplot","jitter"),
log="y")
```

The preceding code results in the following graph (*Figure 2.11*):

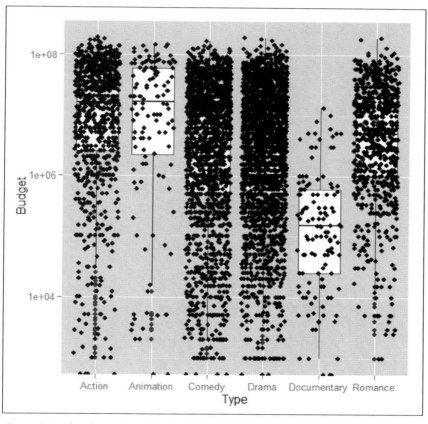

Figure 2.11: This shows the boxplot of movie budgets for different categories of movies, including data points with jittering (y axis in the log scale)

As is clear from the plot we obtained, we are now able to better recognise the position of the individual measurements on the plot. On the other hand, one problem we have now is that the data is almost covering the boxplot, and this is not really what we want. As you already know, we could change the order of the element in the `geom` vector, so that the boxplot would be drawn on top of the jittering measurements, but in this case, we would simply get the box covering the data. One option to overcome this issue would be to have the boxplot on top of the data, but add some transparency to it, so that the data is still visible. In order to do that, we simply use the `alpha` argument we introduced in the *Histogram* section. Just remember that we need to use the `I()` function in order to fix the transparency to a fixed value. The following data shows this:

```
qplot(Type,Budget, data=myMovieData,
geom=c("jitter","boxplot"),alpha=I(0.6), log="y")
```

In *Figure 2.12*, you can see the plot we obtained. Now all the elements are there for a nice visualization of the different budgets. It also shows the individual measurements for each movie type available from the dataset, and which were then used to build the boxplots. For instance, the **Animation** and **Documentary** types have a much smaller sample size compared with the other categories, so we can also assume that the descriptive statistics represented in the boxplot may be less accurate.

The preceding code results in the following graph:

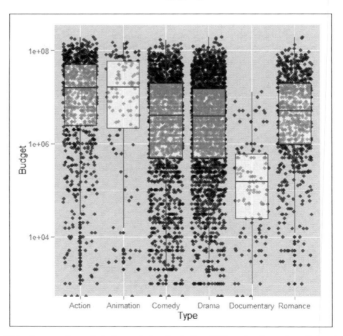

Figure 2.12: This shows a boxplot of movie budgets for different categories of movies, including data points with jittering and transparency on the boxplot (the y axis in the log scale)

Scatterplots

Scatterplots are probably among the most common plots, since they are frequently used to display the relationship between two quantitative variables. When two variables are provided, `ggplot2` will make a scatterplot by default. Now that you have already acquired some experience from the previous sections of this chapter, the representation of the scatter plot will be quite straightforward for you.

For our example on how to build a scatterplot, we will use a dataset called `ToothGrowth`, which is available in the base R installation. Reported in this dataset are measurements of the length of the teeth of 10 guinea pigs for three different doses of vitamin C (0.5, 1, and 2 mg). It is delivered in two different ways—as orange juice or as ascorbic acid (a compound with vitamin C activity). You can find details on the dataset help page at `?ToothGrowth`.

We are interested in seeing how the length of the teeth changed for each different dose. We are not able to distinguish the different guinea pigs since this information is not contained in the data, so for the moment, we will simply plot the data we have:

```
require(ggplot2)
qplot(dose, len, data=ToothGrowth, geom="point")
##Alternative coding
qplot(dose, len, data=ToothGrowth)
```

The resulting plot is reproduced in *Figure 2.13*. As you have seen, the default plot generated, without a `geom` argument, is the scatterplot, which is the default bivariate plot type. In this plot, we see that the length of the teeth increases as the vitamin C intake increases. On the other hand, we know that since the vitamin C was provided in two different ways, as orange juice or as ascorbic acid, it could be interesting to check whether these two groups behave differently.

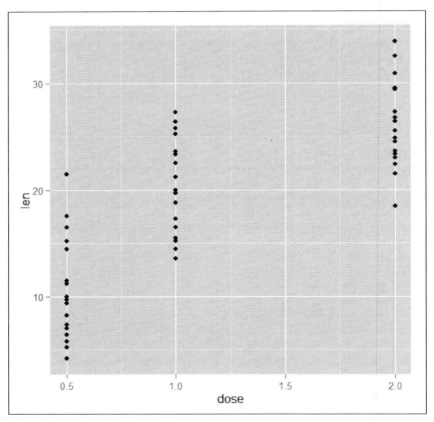

Figure 2.13: This shows a scatterplot of the data on tooth length versus the dose in ToothGrowth

The first approach could be to have the data in two different colors. To do that, we simply need to assign the color attribute to the column `supp` in the data, which defines the way in which vitamin C is given to the guinea pigs:

```
qplot(dose, len,data=ToothGrowth, geom="point", col=supp)
```

The resulting plot is in *Figure 2.14*. We will discuss later on in the book how the colors are assigned in ggplot2, but for now, we will only focus on the general layout. We can now find out which intake route each data point came from, and it looks like the subgroup where orange juice was administered has higher teeth growth compared to the subgroup where ascorbic acid was administered. Nevertheless, to differentiate between them is not easy. We could then try with the facets, so that the data will be completely separated in two different subplots. So let's see what happens:

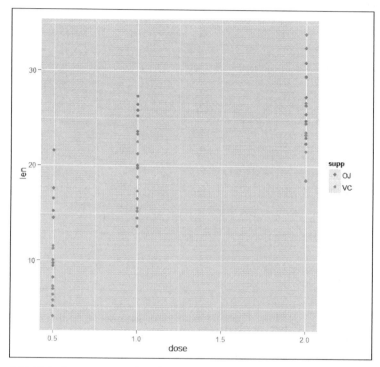

Figure 2.14: This shows a scatterplot of the length of teeth versus the dose in ToothGrowth with data in different colors depending on vitamin C intake

The discussion in the preceding paragraph is encapsulated in this code:

```
qplot(dose, len,data=ToothGrowth, geom="point", facets=.~supp)
```

In this new plot, showed in *Figure 2.15*, we definitely have a better picture of the data, since we can see how the growth of teeth differs for the different intakes.

As illustrated in this simple example, the best visualization can differ depending on the data you have. In some cases, grouping a variable with colors or dividing the data with faceting may give you a different idea about the data and its tendency. For instance, with the plot in *Figure 2.15*, we see that growth of teeth increases with the dose and seems to be each for different intake route. However when studying only the data points, it is difficult to identify any difference in the data behavior:

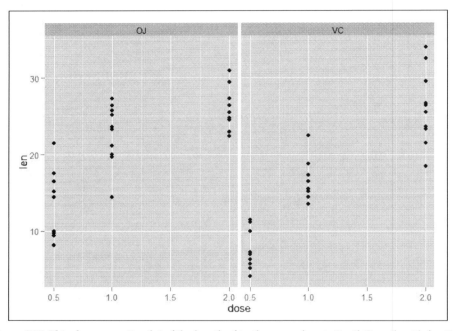

Figure 2.15: This shows a scatterplot of the length of teeth versus dose in ToothGrowth with faceting

One approach to highlighting the general tendency of the data could be to include a smooth line in the graph. In this case, we can see that the growth after the administration of orange juice does not look linear, so a smooth line could be a nice way to capture this. In order to do that, we simply add a smooth curve to the vector of geometry components in the qplot function. The following code shows this:

```
qplot(dose, len,data=ToothGrowth, geom=c("point","smooth"),
facets=.~supp)
```

As you can see from the plot obtained in *Figure 2.16*, we now clearly see, not only the different data thanks to the faceting, but also the tendency of the data with respect to the dose administered. As you have seen, the smooth line in `ggplot2` will also require a confidence interval in the plot. If you don't want the confidence interval, you can simply add the `se=FALSE` argument. We will cover this topic in more detail in *Chapter 4, Advanced Plotting Techniques*.

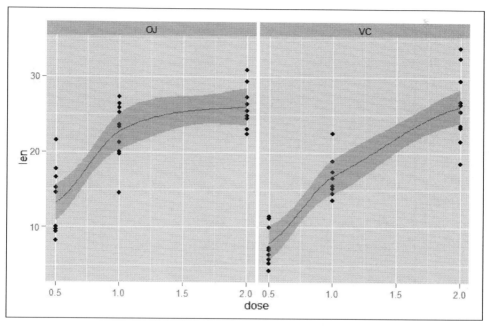

Figure 2.16: This shows a scatterplot of the length of teeth versus the dose in ToothGrowth with faceting and a smooth line

Time series

In this section, we will cover a special case of data you may find in R—the time series. This class of data is used in R to represent time data, such as hours, years, or dates in general. Of the data available in the R installation, there are some datasets containing time series, such as the UKgas and economics datasets. For our simple example, we will use the latter, which is a data frame containing population and employment information in the US over the last 40 years. You can find an overview of the dataset information in the help page at ?economics.

Let's first have a look to the dataset and see its structure:

```
head(economics)
```

	date	pce	pop	psavert	uempmed	unemploy
1	1967-06-30	507.8	198712	9.8	4.5	2944
2	1967-07-31	510.9	198911	9.8	4.7	2945
3	1967-08-31	516.7	199113	9.0	4.6	2958
4	1967-09-30	513.3	199311	9.8	4.9	3143
5	1967-10-31	518.5	199498	9.7	4.7	3066
6	1967-11-30	526.2	199657	9.4	4.8	3018

As illustrated, this data has the usual dataset structure, with the first column of the data containing dates. For such data, you will not need any special modification. For instance, let's plot unemployment versus time in a typical scatterplot. In this case, instead of dots to represent individual data points, we can use a continuous line, so that we will have a continuous description of the data with time. We can simply use qplot as we would do normally, by selecting the two columns we want to plot and choosing the "line" geometry. This is shown in the following code:

```
qplot(date, unemploy, data=economics, geom="line")
```

As you can see in *Figure 2.17*, the plot looks exactly like a normal plot, with the difference that `ggplot2` recognized the time series and represented dates and not simple numbers:

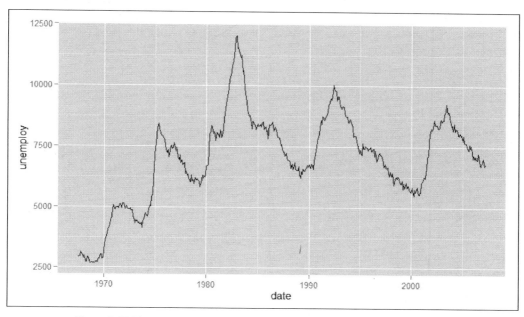

Figure 2.17: This is an example of a time series plot from the economics dataset, representing unemployment versus time

Bubble charts and dot plots

In the scatterplot section, we have seen how bivariate data can be represented in a typical *x-y* plot. In some cases, you may need to represent an additional variable in your plot, and we have already seen how different colors can be used to represent different types of data. One other option is to use the size of the symbols; if you are representing the data in points, you can, for instance, change the point size to represent an additional property of your data (an additional variable). This type of plot is usually called a bubble chart.

We can see a very easy example using the movie dataset we created in the *Bar charts* example. Please refer to that section for how to create this dataset.

We can create a plot of the different types of movies versus time by adding the size attribute of the symbol (in this case, they are points) to represent the budget of the movie. This is an example of the code to generate such a plot:

```
qplot(Year, Type, data=myMovieData, size=Budget)
```

As illustrated in the resulting plot in *Figure 2.18*, without selecting a special geometry the observations are, by default, represented as points.

You can also see how it was possible to generate a bivariate plot, as an *x-y* plot, with one discrete variable—the `movie` type in this case. This type of plot, often called *dot plot*, has the advantage, compared with a boxplot, of showing the progression of the data for each category for different years, while the point size is used to represent the budget of each movie. For instance, in *Figure 2.8*, we were able to show the distribution of budgets for each movie type, but not to differentiate whether budgets had changed over the years, as is the case for many types of movies.

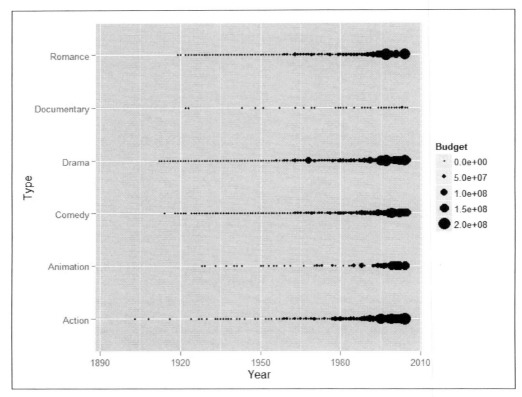

Figure 2.18: This is a dot plot of movie production versus time
with the point size representing the budget amount

Further reading

Additional examples can be found on the respective help pages of each geometric attribute, or on the webpages of the ggplot document. Here are some useful links to such pages:

- The qplot function: http://docs.ggplot2.org/current/qplot.html
- Histograms: http://docs.ggplot2.org/current/geom_histogram.html
- Density plots: http://docs.ggplot2.org/current/geom_density.html and http://docs.ggplot2.org/current/stat_density.html
- Bar charts: http://docs.ggplot2.org/current/geom_bar.html
- Boxplots: http://docs.ggplot2.org/current/geom_boxplot.html
- Scatterplots and Bubble charts: http://docs.ggplot2.org/0.9.3.1/geom_point.html

Summary

In this chapter, we went through the most important plot types that can be realized with ggplot2. We have seen how to realize histograms and density plots, how to build bar charts and boxplots, and how to create scatterplots for bivariate data. Moreover, you saw the application of special types of plots, such as the representation of time series data, as well as bubble charts. For each plot type, you saw simple examples with the inclusion of additional elements in the basic plot, such as faceting and change in point size and color, using the qplot function. In the next chapter, we will start using the more sophisticated ggplot function.

3
The Layers and Grammar of Graphics

In this chapter, we will take a closer look at the grammar of graphics as implemented in ggplot2. We will go through the main concepts of the layer approach that will help you to understand and master the full potential of the basic qplot function which we were introduced to in *Chapter 2, Getting Started*. After a general introduction to the different components of the grammar of graphics, we will go deeper into the faceting, coordinate system, scales, and concept of layers in dedicated sections of this chapter. Afterwards, we will have a look at how you can use the ggplot() function and how its code relates to the one you have already seen used with the simplified qplot() function.

Components of layered grammar

The grammar of graphics is a tool that allows us to effectively describe the components of a graph. In *Chapter 1, Graphics in R*, we mentioned some of the basic concepts behind the approach implemented in ggplot2 for data visualization. The ggplot2 package is an implementation of the ideas presented in the book, *The Grammar of Graphics (Statistics and Computing)* by *Leland Wilkinson*. The goal of the book was to define a set of general unifying principles for the visualization of data. For this reason, the plotting paradigm implemented in the package is based on the idea that, instead of providing many different functions, with each one targeting the realization of one specific type of graph, providing a smaller set of functions defines the different components of a graph and can be combined to generate a large variety of plots.

The grammar of graphics is designed to help in separating and identifying each step of the charting process, helping you to better decide upon the best way to visualize data. Reflecting the structure of a language, each component of the grammar of graphics in `ggplot2` has a specific name, and in *Figure 3.1*, you can find an overall representation of these components:

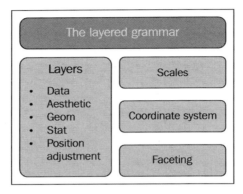

Figure 3.1: This is the overall diagram of the different components of the grammar of graphics as implemented in ggplot2

If we take as an example a simple scatterplot, what we are plotting is one point representing the value of a variable y corresponding to the value of a different variable x. If the values come from different measurements or experiments, we could also group them and represent them with a different color. If, for instance, we look at the `Orange` data, which we introduced in *Chapter 1, Graphics in R*, we have two variables, `age` and `circumference`, and a third variable, `Tree`, identifying the tree from which the measurement was taken. The following code shows this:

```
> head(Orange)
```

The output will be as follows:

	Tree	age	circumference
1	1	118	30
2	1	484	58
3	1	664	87
4	1	1004	115
5	1	1231	120
6	1	1372	142

As mentioned earlier, we could represent the circumference of `trees` (x) against their age (y) and group them by the tree used in the measurement using a different color. These elements, such as the horizontal and vertical position of the points as well as their size, shape, and color, are elements that are perceived in the plot and defined as aesthetic objects. Each aesthetic attribute can also be mapped to a variable to represent a cluster of data or set to a constant value. In this example, that's what we did when mapping the color.

After selecting the data we are interested in representing, we need to choose how to represent them. We could, for instance, use bars, lines connecting the observations, or simply points to represent the observed values on the plot. All these elements (bars, lines, and points) are geometric objects (`geom`) of the graph. They are independent of the data and several of these components could be applied to the same dataset. The next step would be to actually represent the data, but in order to do that, we would need to convert the actual data contained in the dataset in to elements that the computer can represent (for instance, pixels) and elements that can be mapped to aesthetic units, such as the different colors in our example. These transformations are done by the scales. This scaled data can then be represented in the coordinate system on which we want to plot the data. You can see the different components of the plot representation depicted in the simple example in *Figure 3.2*.

As you have seen, to create the complete plot in this simple example, we had to go through different steps:

- The data and the geometric elements are combined with the coordinate system to produce the plot
- Together with the *x-y* variables represented in the plot, additional aesthetic attributes can be assigned, such as the mapping of data to different colors
- Scales are used to transform the data into elements that can be represented and mapped to aesthetic attributes

An additional possibility could be to split the data into different panels in a process defined as faceting or to perform statistical (`stat`) transformation on the data.

Going back to *Figure 3.1*, you can now see how a plot is composed of layers containing information about the data, geometric representation, statistical transformation, and aesthetic elements, for instance. The layers are then combined with scales and the coordinate system to represent the graphics object. Optionally, data can be split into facets. One plot can then contain several layers, for instance, if different geometries overlap (points and boxplot in *Figure 2.12* of *Chapter 2, Getting Started*,) or if statistical transformations are included in the data (smooth line in *Figure 2.16* of *Chapter 2, Getting Started*).

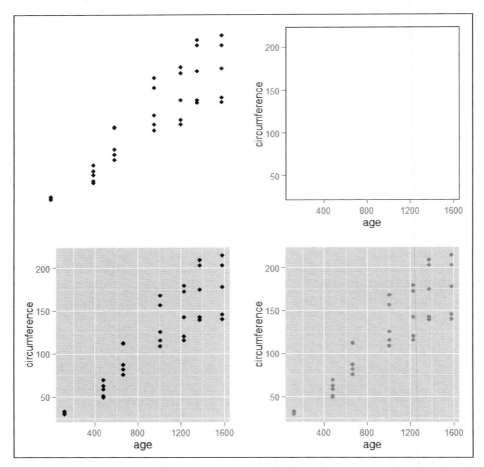

Figure 3.2: This is a representation of the main components of a plot in the grammar of graphics; the data and the geometric elements (top-left corner) are combined with the coordinate system (top-right corner) to obtain the plot (bottom-left corner). Additional aesthetic attributes can be added, for instance, mapping to color to another variable (bottom-right corner)

We will now go into more detail, discussing the different components of the grammar of graphics, as represented in *Figure 3.1*, in the following sections, and we will discuss in more detail the layers and their individual components in the *Layers in ggplot2* section of this chapter.

Creating a plot layer by layer with the ggplot function

We have already seen that `qplot()` is a simple function that can be used to generate plots quickly, but for more detailed control of the plot layers, the `ggplot2` package also provides a more sophisticated function, `ggplot()`. Using this function, we first create a plot object in which we define the data and the aesthetic mapping we are interested in representing, and afterwards, we add elements such as `geom` and stat that produce the actual plot. Just remember that aesthetic mapping not only includes the colors and sizes of plotting elements, but also the *x-y* mapping to the axis. In the previous chapter, we showed an example of creating a scatterplot with the `ToothGrowth` dataset, where it described the effect of vitamin C on tooth growth in guinea pigs. We will now use the same dataset as an example and discuss how you can build the plot in *Figure 2.14* of *Chapter 2, Getting Started* by adding one layer on top of the other.

First of all, we will create our basic plot object containing the data and aesthetic mapping. The following code shows this:

```
myPlot <-ggplot(data=ToothGrowth, aes(x=dose, y=len, col=supp))
```

As illustrated in this case, aesthetic mapping is provided using the `aes()` (aesthetics) function within the body of the `ggplot()` function. If you try to call the object just created, `myPlot`, you will get an empty window and an error message specifying that there is no actual layer in the plot. This object, in fact, contains the basic information of the plot, but it does not produce any output since it does not yet contain any `geom` assignment, so there is no actual visualization attribute assigned to the plot. The `myPlot` object is an R S3 object of the class `ggplot` consisting of a component named `data` and other components containing information about the plot. The plot details contained in such objects can be accessed using the `summary()` function. The following code shows this:

```
summary(myPlot)
```

The output will be as follows:

```
data: len, supp, dose [60x3]
mapping:  x = dose, y = len, color = supp
faceting: facet_null()
```

As illustrated, in this way we can keep track of exactly which data was used in the plot and how the mapping was realized; this is particularly useful if you save the plot objects in your workspace and then would like to check their content.

So, let's now add a layer to our basic plot object and create a basic plot. As we will see in the *Layers in ggplot2* section, a basic plot can be realized using data, aesthetic mapping, and geometry, so in this case, we are only missing this last component. In the ggplot() function, additional layers can be added using the + operator followed by the function defining the layer to be added. So, for a scatterplot with points, we have the following code:

```
myPlot + geom_point()
```

How to separate code in multiple lines

When you use the + operator to add plot elements, you may end up with quite long lines of code which would benefit some organizations. One common way to structure code is by dividing it into multiple lines; just keep in mind that the + operator should be always on the right-hand side of the previous line so you could divide the preceding code into two lines, for instance, in this way:

```
myPlot +
geom_point()
```

In this case, we used the object created previously and which contained the plot information, and added the geometry; one other option is to use all the code together:

```
ggplot(data=ToothGrowth, aes(x=dose, y=len, col=supp)) + geom_point()
```

With both options, you will obtain the same results. Using assignment to objects can be useful, in particular if you have a long series of plots pointing to the same data. In this case, you would have shorter and cleaner code that recalls a previously created plot object.

Also, in this case, we could create a new object, this time containing the final plot, and again using the summary() function, we can get access to its content. The following code shows this:

```
myNewPlot <- myPlot +geom_point()
summary(myNewPlot)
```

The output will be as follows:

```
data: len, supp, dose [60x3]
mapping:  x = dose, y = len, color = supp
faceting: facet_null()
-----------------------------------
geom_point: na.rm = FALSE
stat_identity:
position_identity: (width = NULL, height = NULL)
```

You have seen how all the main details of the plot are accessible, in particular the geom and stat details used.

The layers created can also be overwritten, so, for instance, we can take away the aesthetic mapping of colors on the supp variable. This can be easily done by setting the aesthetic argument col to NULL. The following code shows this:

```
myNewPlot + geom_point(aes(col=NULL))
```

As illustrated in the resulting plot represented in *Figure 3.3*, we overwrote the aesthetic of color assignment, but the legend, which was created with the previous call, is still present since the legend represents the aesthetic scale that was generated in the first layer by calling myNewPlot, which contains the aesthetic assignment. These examples show us how aesthetic mapping applied to a layer only affect that layer, while scales and legends will remain at their default values unless manually modified.

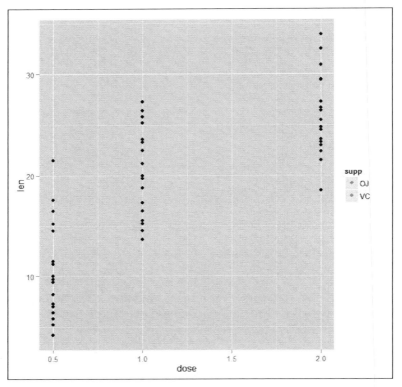

Figure 3.3: This is an example of color aesthetic mapping overwritten without overwriting the legend argument

In order to take away the legend in this example, we will have to overwrite that component directly with the following code:

```
myNewPlot + geom_point(aes(col=NULL)) +
theme(legend.position="none")
```

In these latest examples, we have seen something very important concerning `ggplot2` and the way the plotting is implemented. In fact, in this graphical package the plots can be saved as R objects, which can then be called to produce the visualization of the graph and stored within the workspace. More importantly, these objects can also be used to produce new plots by updating the layers that compose the original picture. This is a very useful functionality that differentiates `ggplot2` from the paradigm implemented in other graphical packages such as `graphics` or `lattice`.

Scales

Scales take care of the mapping of aesthetic attributes to the data. When the data is assigned to aesthetic mapping, the scales map the data to the corresponding aesthetic attribute, and this is done via a specific function depending on the scale applied. The inverse of this function is then used to map back the elements from the aesthetic to the actual value of the data. This process is used to create the axis, to represent the x-y position of the elements on the plot, or to create the legends that represent the mapping of other aesthetic attributes.

If, for instance, we consider the assignment of data to a color scale. First, the data is assigned to a color by mapping the value of the data to colors within the range defined by the scale, and then the inverse of the scale defines the total range of colors used in the mapping, which will be used to draw the legend of the graph.

Within a plot, each aesthetic assignment has a different scale, and each aesthetic attribute has a default scale assigned. After the scale is assigned to an aesthetic, the same scale is applied to that specific aesthetic on all the data in the plot in order to guarantee consistent mapping.

In the following *Figure 3.4*, you will find some examples of scales depicted. As illustrated, scales will appear slightly different if they apply to scatterplots, with point geometry or if they apply to the filling of histograms, for instance. In ggplot2, you have access to color scales in the continuous range, which can be used to map continuous variables. Finally, we also have the possibility of mapping variables to the size or shape of the symbols used in the plot. We will cover the topic of scales in more detail in *Chapter 5, Controlling Plot Details*, so for now, it is only important that you have an idea of the different possibilities available in ggplot2.

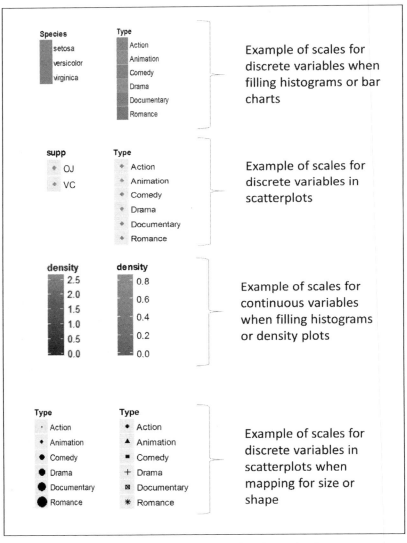

Figure 3.4: These are a few examples of typical scales

The coordinate system

The coordinate system adjusts the mapping from coordinates to the 2D plane of the computer screen. Among the different coordinate systems available in `ggplot2`, the Cartesian system is the most common coordinate system for two dimensions, while the polar coordinate system is often used for special plots, such as pie charts. When you create a plot, the coordinate system for the graph will be set with default values, which, in most cases, would be Cartesian coordinates. If you want a different coordinate system, you can overwrite the default value using the appropriate function. Such functions have the general form `coord_x`, where *x* is replaced by the specific coordinate desired.

The following is a table summarizing the main functions of coordinate systems; a more exhaustive list can be found on the package website:

Main coord functions	Description
`coord_cartesian(xlim, ylim)`	This is a Cartesian coordinate system. `xlim` and `ylim` can be used to provide limits for the axis. They are provided as vectors indicating the range.
`coord_fixed(ratio , xlim , ylim)`	These are Cartesian coordinates with a fixed relationship between the *x* and *y* scales. The ratio argument defines the ratio between the two axes expressed as *y/x*.
`coord_flip(...)`	This flips the Cartesian coordinates by inverting the *x* and *y* axes.
`coord_polar(theta , start , direction)`	These are polar coordinates. The `theta` argument is used to define the variable to which the map should be mapped; it can be *x* or *y*. `start` is used for the offset of the starting point from twelve o´clock. It is expressed in radians. `direction` can be 1 (clockwise) or -1 (counterclockwise).

We will now see a couple of examples of how to use a few of these functions. We will first have a look at the `coord_flip()` function which simply changes the axes of the plot. In most cases, you will not need any additional argument, so for instance, if we consider the plot in *Figure 2.14*, representing the data from the `ToothGrowth` dataset, we have already seen in the previous section how we can obtain the same plot defining the different layers with `ggplot()`. If now, we want to flip the coordinates, we simply need to change the coordinate system. The following code shows this:

```
ggplot(data=ToothGrowth, aes(x=dose, y=len, col=supp)) +
geom_point() + coord_flip()
```

This code will create the plot in *Figure 3.5*, where the *x* and *y* axes are flipped compared to the default coordinates:

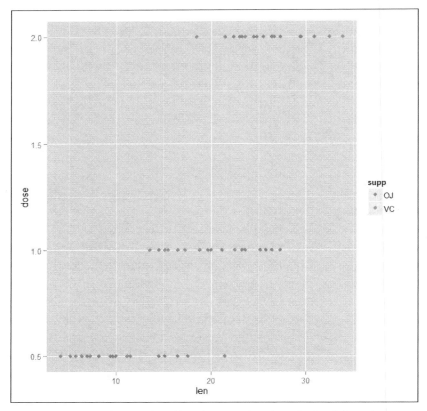

Figure 3.5: This is a plot of length versus dose from the ToothGrowth dataset with an inverted coordinate system

One other very useful function is the `coord_fixed()` function which allows us to create a plot with a fixed ratio of the *y* and *x* axes. The default value for the ratio argument is 1 which creates a plot with the same fixed axis extension for *x* and *y*, ensuring that one unit on the *x* axis is the same length as one unit on the *y* axis. Just remember that this does not mean that the two axes will have the same range but simply that the unit extension would be the same.

So, for instance, if we take the plot in our previous example, we could, instead of flipping the coordinates, set them to a fixed value. The following code shows this:

```
ggplot(data=ToothGrowth, aes(x=dose, y=len, col=supp)) +
geom_point() + coord_fixed(ratio=0.1)
```

In this case, we have fixed the ratio of the two axes to `0.1`, meaning that one length unit on the *x* axis will be translated to 10 units on the *y* axis. The plot generated with the previous code is represented in *Figure 3.6*:

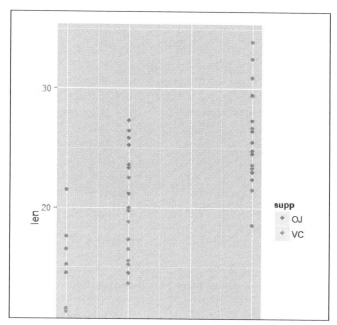

Figure 3.6: This shows a plot of length versus dose from the ToothGrowth dataset using a fixed coordinate system with a ratio of 0.1 for y/x

Faceting

Faceting is a mechanism to automatically lay out multiple plots on one page. This functionality is quite nice and useful in many situations and, for this reason, we will venture a little deeper into it and look at some examples. As already mentioned, if you are familiar with other plotting packages, this functionality is very similar to the concept of `panels` in `lattice`.

The plot is realized with the faceting option by splitting the data into subsets, and each subset of data is represented in an individual plot. Nevertheless, the individual plots are formatted in an overall plot page with a header at the top or on the side of the panels, which identify the data represented in the subplot. Faceting is particularly useful if you need to have a first impression of how different data sets behaves or if the representation of the data should be separated for any reason.

There are two main ways to perform faceting in `ggplot2`: grid faceting and wrap faceting.

Grid faceting

This is probably the faceting you will use most of the time. Grid faceting consists of creating a faceting of the plot by splitting the data into subgroups relative to two or more variables, which are then used to produce subplots for the specific combinations of variables. In grid faceting, at least two variables are provided and if you are interested in splitting the graph by only one variable, the second one is replaced by a . (dot), indicating that all variables should be taken for the second splitting. Let's start with a simple example. We will work on the `myMovieData` dataset, which we created in *Chapter 2*, *Getting Started*, starting with the movies dataset available in R. We will work with the `ggplot()` function, so you can already begin to become familiar with this other function. In order to add grid faceting to a plot, we will use the `facet_grid()` function. The first argument of the function is the faceting elements and hence the variables for which we want to create facet plots. For instance, we could use `facet_grid(x~y)`, indicating that we have one row for each value of the variable x and one column for each value of the variable y. If we were only interested in a split by the variable x, we would code it as `facet_wrap(x~.)`, indicating that the variable represented in the plot will only be split by x in rows and all other subsets will be included in the plot. Similarly, the `facet_grid(.~.)` code will not produce any faceting.

Now, let's go to our example. We can now plot the histogram of movie budgets by splitting the data by budget. We will also plot the budget in the log scale in order to make the distribution clearer; you can also obtain the same result by just using the `log()` function on the budget variable, but in the example, you will also see the alternative function available in `ggplot2`. You have the possibility of splitting in to columns or rows, and as illustrated, they produce a result that is visually very different.

```
### Faceting with orientation by rows
ggplot(data=myMovieData,aes(Budget)) + geom_histogram(binwith=1) +
facet_grid(Type~.) + scale_x_log10()
```

```
### Faceting with orientation by columns
ggplot(data=myMovieData,aes(Budget)) + geom_histogram(binwith=1) +
facet_grid(.~Type)+ scale_x_log10()
```

The answer to the question as to which orientation of the plot better describes the data really depends on the distribution you are representing and the range of the data. For instance, if the range in x is much larger than the one in y, splitting by rows would often give you a much better visualization. In this specific case, the orientation of faceting by columns seems more adequate. In *Figure 3.7*, you can see the resulting graphs generated with the two different visualization options:

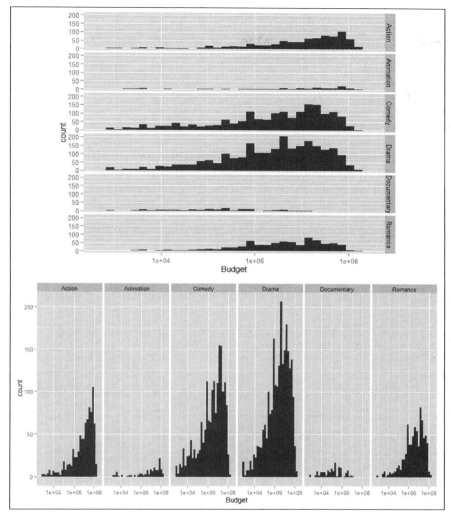

Figure 3.7: This shows the histogram of movie budget faceting by movie type.
The faceting is done by rows (top graph) or by columns (bottom graph)

As already discussed, we can also generate plots by splitting by two different
variables, so in this case it would be interesting to have a look at the movie budgets
split by years and movie type. We have quite a few different years in the dataset—
more than 100. Now, 100 plots would be quite difficult to visualize. So first of all,
we will add a column to our dataset, rounding off the years of the movies to their
decades. We can do that, for instance, by rounding the years to just three significant
digits. The following code shows this:

```
myMovieData$roundYear <- signif(myMovieData$Year, digits = 3)
```

This new column will group the movies around the closest decade in which they were made, so, for instance, the 1980s decade will include movies from 1975 up to 1984.

We will use the column just created to have the histogram split by decade:

```
ggplot(data=myMovieData,aes(Budget)) + geom_histogram(binwith=1) +
facet_grid(roundYear~Type) + scale_x_log10()
```

In *Figure 3.8*, you can see the resulting picture. In this case, we produced a matrix plot with rows and columns representing the possible combinations of the two variables: decades and movie type. You can also see how this visualization includes all the possible combinations between these two variables even if there is no data, so you can notice how, in some cases, the subplot could be empty.

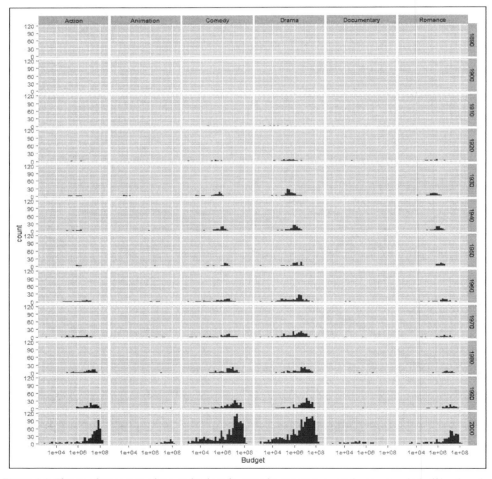

Figure 3.8: This is a histogram of movie budget faceting by movie type and year rounded off by decades

One very useful argument of the `facet_grid()` function is the margin option. In this argument it is possible to provide additional facets that could be added to the plot. These additional facets can be provided as a vector of names listing the variables for which facets should be produced or as a logical vector, where TRUE indicates the creation of additional facets containing all the data. We will see an example of this option, which will add an additional column and row to the plot in *Figure 3.8* where the distributions for all the data are represented:

```
ggplot(data=myMovieData,aes(Budget)) + geom_histogram(binwith=1) +
facet_grid(roundYear~Type, margin=TRUE) + scale_x_log10()
```

The resulting plot is represented in *Figure 3.9*. As you can see, the intersection between columns and rows of all the data represents the budget distribution for all the data:

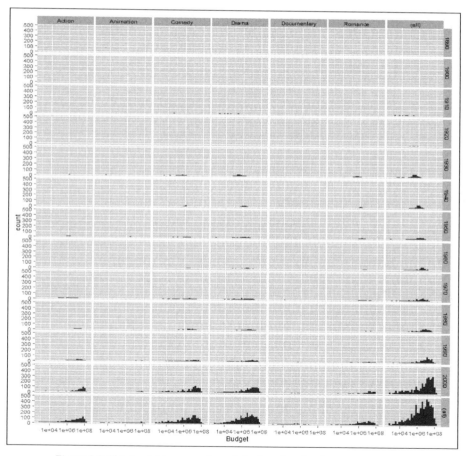

Figure 3.9: This is a histogram of movie budget faceting by movie type and year rounded off by decades containing a facet for all the data

Using the faceting option, it is also possible to produce facets for more than two variables. This can be done using the + operator to add additional variables to the row or column argument of the faceting. For instance, in our example, we could perform faceting for year and movie type—all by columns. In this case, to reduce the number of plots, we could look only at the movies after the 1980s. Also notice how only a subset of the data is used within the plot function. The following code shows this:

```
ggplot(data=subset(myMovieData, roundYear>1980),
aes(Budget)) +
geom_histogram(binwith=1) +
facet_grid(.~Type+roundYear) + s
cale_x_log10()
```

The resulting plot is showed in *Figure 3.10*. For instance, this kind of visualization would allow you to have the movie budgets for both the 1990s and the 2000s for each type of movie side by side, allowing easy comparison of the distribution of the budgets in these two different decades. As you can see, in this example, we have also used the subset() function directly within the plot function to choose only a subset of the data. Such an approach may turn out to be very useful in some cases.

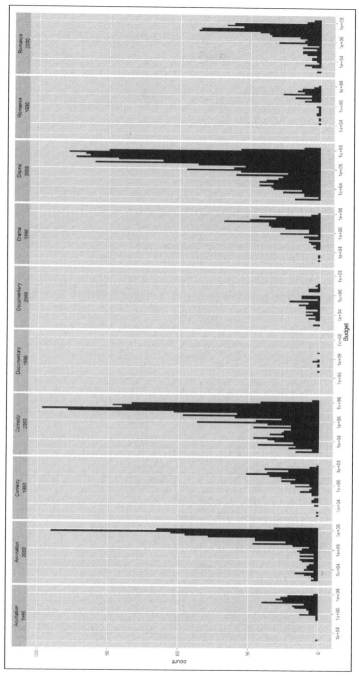

Figure 3.10: This is a histogram of movie budget faceting by movie type and the decades 1990s and 2000s with facets by columns

Wrap faceting

Wrap faceting produces a single ribbon of plots that are spread along one or more rows. This kind of faceting is particularly useful if you have faceting with many combinations; here the subplots can be arranged in several rows, making the plot much easier to read. To realize wrap faceting, we can use the `facet_wrap()` function. We will see a simple example using our simplified `movie` dataset. We will look at the movie budgets for each year from 2000 onwards. This will generate a relatively large series of plots, and wrap faceting will help us to have better representation of the data. The following code shows this:

```
ggplot(data=subset(myMovieData,Year>1999),
aes(Budget)) +
geom_histogram() + facet_wrap(~Year, nrow=2) +
scale_x_log10()
```

You can see the resulting plot in *Figure 3.11*.

As illustrated in the previous code, we used the `facet_wrap()` function in which we specified only one variable. This function uses arguments in the form of `facet_wrap(~x+y+z)`, where the faceting variables can be listed. In this case, we can only provide arguments after the ~ sign. We can also specify the number of columns and rows we want to have in the faceting using the `nrow` and `ncol` arguments.

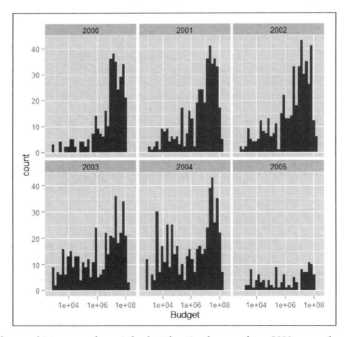

Figure 3.11: This shows a histogram of movie budget faceting by year from 2000 onwards using wrap faceting

Layers in ggplot2

As just discussed in the previous section, we saw how important the concept of layers was when creating a plot with `ggplot2`. These layers are then combined with a coordinate system and other transformations which then generate the final plot. But what exactly are the layers? In the grammar of graphics as implemented in `ggplot2`, the layers are responsible for the objects that we see in the graph. Each layer can come from a different dataset, have different geometry, and have a different aesthetic mapping. As you can see in *Figure 3.1*, the layers are composed of several components—the `data`, `aesthetic`, `geom`, `stat`, and `position adjustment`. Not all these components are needed in order to create a layer, but a minimal layer can be created just by including the data, aesthetic mapping, and `geom` that will define the type of plot to be generated. In fact, the geometry is a very important component of the layer since no visualization is possible without specifying the geometry.

Data

As you can see, the data represents the actual data shown in the plot. At this point, `ggplot2` contains a major restriction compared with other plotting packages in R— the data must be a data frame. This means that even if you have your observations as vector for instance, you would first need to combine them in a data frame and then realize the plot. The reason for this is to ensure that the data used in the plots can be easily traced back, even to people other than the author. Moreover, structuring the data in data frames somehow forces the user to keep it organized, thus reducing the possibility of mistakes and errors.

You should also keep in mind that when you create a data object, the data is copied within the object, so if you change something in the data, the change will not appear in the plot unless you create the plot object again. This is particularly important since `ggplot2` objects can be saved in variables or stored in a workspace, so you should pay attention that the plot is actually updated with changes in data when you save and load `ggplot2` objects.

Aesthetic mapping

As you saw in the examples presented previously in this chapter, aesthetic mapping is provided via the `aes()` function, which can be used, for instance, for x and y mapping, color mapping, or size and shape mapping. All the variables mapped should be present in the data provided, and if mapping is performed within the `geom` or `stat` function, the data should be specified even within the body of the function.

> **Aesthetic mapping to x and y**
>
> When working with aesthetic mapping, keep in mind that even the mapping to the *x* and *y* variables in the plot is a part of aesthetic mapping, and, for this reason, it must be included in the `aes()` functions.

When discussing scales, we described how scales were used for mapping aesthetic arguments such as the *x-y* position in the axes. In the case of color, we can have continuous mapping, where different color levels are mapped to a continuous scale of variables, or we can even have discrete mapping, where the levels of a categorical variable are mapped to different colors. You can see examples of such scales in *Figure 3.4*. When colors are mapped to a categorical variable, the continuous scale of colors is used to select the specific value of a color, which is mapped to the variables. These colors are, by default, selected as equally spaced from the so-called color wheel, represented in *Figure 3.12*:

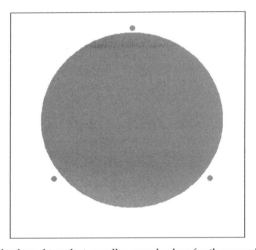

Figure 3.12: This is a color wheel used to select equally spaced colors for the mapping to categorical covariates. Three equally spaced colors assigned by default in ggplot2 are also shown on the outside of the wheel

The default color scheme is selected using the `scale_color_hue()` function, which uses the `hue_pal` function from the scales package to assign the selected color. Calling this function allows you to find the actual color used in the plot by default; this can turn out to be quite useful if you need to reproduce a color assigned by default in a plot. For instance, if you want to know the first three colors of the series, you can use the following code:

```
library(scales)
scales::hue_pal()(3)
```

The output will be as follows:

```
[1] "#F8766D" "#00BA38" "#619CFF"
```

In *Figure 3.12*, you can see where these colors are located with respect to the color wheel and how they are actually equally spaced starting from the twelve o'clock position on the wheel.

The aesthetic attributes that you can map to variables depend on the geom function used. In the following table, you can find the arguments, mandatory and optional, associated with the most important geom functions. As you can easily imagine, the *x* and/or *y* arguments are often mandatory, but the optional arguments are also interesting since those are the arguments you can use to personalize your plot and to shape it in the best way to describe the data you have. Among such arguments, you will find, for instance, the fill argument we used to color the internal part of the histograms or the alpha argument we used for transparency. You can use this table as a reference to quickly search for such arguments and to have a look at the possible alternatives that could be provided by different functions:

Main geom functions	Mandatory aesthetic	Optional aesthetic
geom_abline		alpha, color, linetype, size
geom_area	*x*, ymax (ymin fix to 0)	alpha, color, fill, linetype, size
geom_bar	*x*	alpha, color, fill, linetype, size, weight
geom_boxplot	lower, middle, upper, ymax, ymin	*x*, alpha, color, fill, linetype, shape, size, weight
geom_density	*x*, *y*	alpha, color, fill, linetype, size, weight
geom_dotplot	*x*, *y*	alpha, color, fill
geom_histogram	*x*	alpha, color, fill, linetype, size, weight
geom_hline		alpha, color, linetype, size
geom_jitter	*x*, *y*	alpha, color, fill, shape, size
geom_line	*x*, *y*	alpha, color, linetype, size
geom_point	*x*, *y*	alpha, color, fill, shape, size
geom_ribbon	*x*, ymax, ymin	alpha, color, fill, linetype, size
geom_smooth	*x*, *y*	alpha, color, fill, linetype, size, weight
geom_text	label, *x*, *y*	alpha, angle, color, family, fontface, hjust, lineheight, size, vjust

Geometric

The geometry attributes define the actual type of plot that will be applied to the data provided with the `ggplot()` function. These attributes are provided using functions with the general form `geom_x`, where x can be replaced by the specified geometry, such as, for instance, `histogram` or `point`. Additionally, different data can be used by providing a new dataset to the `geom` function. It is also possible to combine different geometries by combining different functions with the + operator, for instance, `geom_point() + geom_smooth()`.

How to find the names of geom functions

When using `ggplot2` in your coding, it can happen that you won't remember all the names of the `geom` functions, particularly if you need a special functionality you are not familiar with. Obviously, you can use the table provided by this book or have a look at the `ggplot2` website, but one trick that can turn out to be useful is the use of the `apropos()` function available in R to search for a function by a string contained in the function name. So, for instance, using the following code will list all the functions with the `"geom"` string in their name.

```
apropos("geom")
```

Of course, a similar approach could also be used to search for the `"stat"` and `"coord"` functions.

In the following table, you will find a reference to the most important `geom` functions available in `ggplot2`, with a short description indicating the actual plot generated by the function. You can also find the default statistical transformation executed by the function for each function. Pay attention to this argument because if you need a different statistical transformation, you would need to change this argument. You will find more details about statistical transformations in the next section.

Here's the table we talked about:

Main geom functions	Default stat	Description
geom_abline	abline	This is a line specified by the slope and intercept.
geom_area	identity	This is an area plot, which is a continuous analogue of a stacked bar chart. It is a special case of geom_ribbon.
geom_bar	bin	These are bars with bases on the x axis.
geom_blank	identity	This is blank and doesn't draw anything.
geom_boxplot	boxplot	This is a box-and-whiskers plot.
geom_density	density	This is a smooth density estimate calculated by stat_density.
geom_dotplot	bindot	This is a dot plot (the width of a dot corresponds to the bin width and each dot represents one observation).
geom_errorbar	identity	These add error bars to plots by coupling with other geometries.
geom_errorbarh	identity	These are horizontal error bars.
geom_histogram	bin	This is a histogram.
geom_hline	hline	This is a horizontal line.
geom_jitter	identity	These are points jittered (usually to reduce overplotting).
geom_line	identity	These connect observations ordered by the x value.
geom_path	identity	These connect observations in their original order.
geom_point	identity	This represents observations as points, as in a scatterplot.
geom_pointrange	identity	This is an interval represented by a vertical line, with a point in the middle.
geom_ribbon	identity	This is a ribbon of the y range with continuous x values.
geom_smooth	smooth	These add a smoothed conditional mean.
geom_text	identity	These are textual annotations.
geom_tile	identity	This is a tile plane with rectangles.
geom_vline	vline	This is a vertical line.

Stat

A statistical transformation or `stat` is a statistical manipulation applied to the data, usually to summarize the data. A simple example would be the `stat_bin()` transformation which summarizes the data in bins typically for representation in a histogram. The general structure of these functions is `"stat_x"`, where *x* can be replaced by the statistical transformation.

As you have seen in the previous table, each geometry comes with a default statistical transformation that is applied to the data. You would wonder why your data should be statistically manipulated if you only need a typical *x-y* plot, but among the statistical transformations, there is also the identity transformation which basically means that the data is left unchanged. This is usually the transformation applied to `geom`, for which an actual transformation is not needed. With this approach, in `ggplot2`, it is always possible to have a connection between the `geom` and `stat` arguments, keeping the code structure coherent and at the same time providing high flexibility since you can always change the default `stat` argument and generate new plots.

What statistical transformations do is basically take the data provided for the plot, apply the transformation, and return a new dataset, which is then used in the plot (as mentioned, the `stat_identity()` function does not do anything). Depending on the stat applied, this new dataset could contain new variables as outputs of applied statistical transformation. In the following table, you will find a summary of the main `stat` functions with a short description and a the list of new variables created in the transformation. These new variables are pretty interesting since they can also be mapped to aesthetic attributes in the plot. We will see a few examples of how to do this in *Chapter 4, Advanced Plotting Techniques*.

Main stat functions	New variables created	Description
stat_bin	count, density, ncount, ndensity	These split data into bins for histograms.
stat_bindot	*x, y*, binwidth, count, ncount, density, ndensity	These split data into bins for dot plots.
stat_boxplot	width, ymin, lower, notchlower, middle, notchupper, upper, ymax	This calculates the components of a box-and-whiskers plot.
stat_density	density, count, scaled	These calculate the kernel density estimate for a density plot (geom_density).
stat_function	*x, y*	These superimpose a function to the plot.

Main stat functions	New variables created	Description
stat_identity		These plot data without any statistical transformation.
stat_quantile	quantile	These calculate continuous quantiles.
stat_smooth	y, ymin, ymax, se	These add a smoother line.
stat_sum	n, prop	This is the sum of unique values. This is useful for plotting on scatterplots.
stat_summary	fun.data, fun.ymin, fun.y, fun. ymax	These summarise y values at every unique x value.
stat_unique		These remove duplicates.

Position adjustment

Position adjustments are used to adjust the position of each geom. These adjustments do not refer to formatting the legend, axes, titles, and other similar components of the plot; they apply only to the elements in the plot area, such as bars in a bar plot and points in a scatterplot, and they can be applied to continuous and categorical data. As for the stat function, even in this case, we have the position_identity() function which does not adjust the position and which is used if there is no need for any adjustment.

Position adjustment of categorical data

These kinds of adjustments are more commonly used. They are often applied to bar plots in order to adjust the position of the bars. We have already seen an example of such an adjustment in *Figure 2.7* in *Chapter 2, Getting Started*. There are different kinds of adjustments available:

- **Dodge**: It is done using the position_dodge() function. In this adjustment, the bars in a bar plot are placed next to each other for each category.

- **Fill**: It is realized with the position_fill() function. In this adjustment, the objects are overlapped on top of each other and standardized to have the same height, so in a bar plot, bars of the same category are stacked upon one another and the heights are equalized, so the bars would represent proportions and not absolute numbers of frequency.

- **Stack**: It is done with the position_stack() function. It is the same as fill but without the height standardisation. Stacking is the default behavior in many area plots, such as bar plots.

We will now recreate the same plots as in *Figure 2.7* of *Chapter 2, Getting Started* by using the `ggplot()` function and the position adjustment functions so you will have a reference on how to use these functions we have just introduced. The position adjustment specification is provided within the geom function for which position adjustment should be applied. In order to do that, you can simply specify the position desired to the position argument of the geom function. This is the easier way to use position adjustment and, in this case, you will use the default specification of each `position_x` function. The following code shows this:

```
ggplot(data=myMovieData, aes(x=Type,fill=factor(Short)))
 + geom_bar(position="stack")
```

```
ggplot(data=myMovieData, aes(x=Type,fill=factor(Short)))
 + geom_bar(position="dodge")
```

```
ggplot(data=myMovieData, aes(x=Type,fill=factor(Short)))
 + geom_bar(position="fill")
```

If, on the other hand, you want to provide specifications different to the default values, you can use position functions as in the following example:

```
ggplot(data=myMovieData, aes(x=Type,fill=factor(Short))) +
geom_bar(position=position_dodge(width = 0.5))
```

Position adjustment of continuous data

There is only one position adjustment for continuous data, and that is jittering. We have already seen an example of jittering in *Figure 2.12* of *Chapter 2, Getting Started*, jittering as a position adjustment is performed by the `position_jitter()` function. However, since jitter is the default position adjustment in the `geom_jitter()` function, in most cases, if you want to realize the jittering of data, you can simply use the `geom_jitter()` function. On the other hand, if you need to specify parameters different to the default values, then you will need to use the `position_jitter()` function.

Equivalent coding between qplot and ggplot

In this section, we will have a look at how we can realize a few of the plots we introduced in *Chapter 2, Getting Started*, with the `ggplot()` function we have introduced in this chapter. The idea is that you can use this simple roadmap as guidance on how to use the `ggplot()` function to generate several kinds of plots, building on the knowledge of `qplot()` that you already have. We will not go into too much detail about the different plots since many basic concepts have already been introduced in the previous chapter and they apply to both functions.

In the following examples, we will use a few of the `geom` and `stat` functions listed in the summary tables previously presented; just remember that for each of these functions, you can map different aesthetic attributes. You can find a list of such attributes in the summary tables or in the help page of the function.

Histograms and density plots

In order to obtain a histogram, we will use the `ggplot()` function to create the aesthetic assignments to the dataset and the `geom_histogram` function to assign the geometry that creates the actual histogram. You will see how this is the general framework of how we can use the `ggplot()` function to create plots. The same process applies to the density plot, with the `geom` function being the only difference.

In this first example, you can also see the corresponding code with the `qplot()` function, while for the next example, we will stick to the code of the `ggplot()` function. The following code will produce the same plot as in *Figure 2.4* of *Chapter 2, Getting Started*:

```
#### Example with the qplot() function
qplot(Petal.Length, data=iris, geom="histogram", color=Species,
fill=Species, alpha=I(0.5))


qplot(Petal.Length, data=iris, geom="density", color=Species,
fill=Species, alpha=I(0.5))


#### Example with the ggplot() function
ggplot(data=iris, aes(x=Petal.Length,color=Species,fill=Species)) +
geom_histogram(alpha=I(0.5))


ggplot(data=iris, aes(x=Petal.Length,color=Species,fill=Species)) +
geom_density(alpha=I(0.5))
```

You will also notice how the aesthetic assignments of position (only *x* in this case) and color are provided in the `ggplot()` function since they can also be applied to the overall plot, while the alpha aesthetic attribute, which applies directly to the histogram, is provided in the `geom` function. Since we do not make further use of the data other than to produce the histogram, the `ggplot()` function simply has the function of initializing the plot object. So, in this case, we could also alternatively provide all the arguments in the `geom` function, as shown in the following code:

```
ggplot() + geom_histogram(data=iris,
aes(x=Petal.Length,color=Species,fill=Species),alpha=I(0.5))
```

Nevertheless, I would not recommend that you use this kind of coding since it can be more difficult to read.

Bar charts

We will now use the `ggplot()` function to create the plot represented in *Figure 2.6.* of *Chapter 2, Getting Started*. In order to do that, we need our `myMovieData` dataset which we used in *Chapter 2, Getting Started*.

```
ggplot(data=myMovieData, aes(x=Type,fill=factor(Short))) + geom_bar()
```

As illustrated even in this second example, when using `ggplot()` instead of `qplot()`, you simply need to remember that the aesthetic must be provided using the `aes()` function within the body of the `ggplot()` function, while the geometry of the plot must be provided using the dedicated `geom` function. So, this implies that for a traditional plot, that is, in `qplot()`, you would start by specifying the *x* and *y* attributes at the beginning of the function, while in `ggplot()` you should keep in mind that those assignments are aesthetic assignments, so they are performed with the other aesthetic attributes.

Boxplots

To show you an example of boxplot, we will reproduce *Figure 2.12* of *Chapter 2, Getting Started*. In this case, you will also see how to combine different geometries since we will need to combine the boxplot with the jitter geometry. The following code shows this:

```
ggplot(data=myMovieData,
aes(Type,Budget)) +
geom_jitter() + geom_boxplot(alpha=I(0.6)) +
scale_y_log10()
```

As illustrated in the jitter geometry defined by the `geom_jitter()` function, we do not need to specify any argument since it applies to all the arguments already specified in the `ggplot()` function. On the other hand, for the boxplot geometry, we need to specify the transparencies with the alpha argument. Also, in this case, as already described for the `qplot()` function in this corresponding example, the order of the `geom` functions will determine the order of drawing the plot components, so if you draw the boxplot first and then the jittered observations, they would cover the plot. Finally, in this example, you also saw the appearance of the first scale argument. As mentioned, scales are dedicated to the mapping of the data to the aesthetic arguments, and the *x-y* position is among the aesthetic arguments, so in order to change the axis to a log scale, we need to change the scale used to draw the plot. This is done by overwriting the default layer of the plot (the default scale) using the dedicated scale function. We will go into more detail about the different scales and their relative functions in *Chapter 5, Controlling Plot Details*.

Scatterplots

In this example, we will recreate *Figure 2.16* of *Chapter 2, Getting Started* using the new functions that you learned about in this chapter. Here, we will represent the data of our `ToothGrowth` dataset as points, but we will split them into different facets depending on the supplement used to administer vitamin C, and we will also add a smooth line. You have already seen in the *Faceting* section how to split the data by faceting, but in this example, you will see how to add statistics to the plot, which, in this case, is the smooth line, and also how to combine the different components: geometry of points, statistics, and faceting. The following code shows this:

```
ggplot(data=ToothGrowth, aes(x=dose,
y=len)) + geom_point() +
stat_smooth() + facet_grid(.~supp)
```

As illustrated, we combined the different components in a way similar to the previous examples. You simply need to add the different functions on the plot created by `ggplot()`. In the `geom` or `stat` function, you can then provide additional arguments, which, in this example, were not needed.

Further reading

- *The Grammar of Graphics (Statistics and Computing) (2nd edition),*
  L. Wilkinson, Springer
- *The PhD thesis, Practical Tools for Exploring Data and Models, H. Wickham*

Summary

In this chapter, you saw the basics of the grammar of graphics as implemented in `ggplot2` and how the concept of layer is used in the process of building the graph. You saw the high-level components of a plot such as the scales, coordinate system, and faceting, and you went through some examples of these functionalities. You then explored the concept of layer by reading descriptions of the different components of a layer. In the examples shown, you had the chance to see the basic use of the `ggplot()` function, which will be the basis for building more advanced examples.

4
Advanced Plotting Techniques

In this chapter, we will explore a few of the more advanced features and plots that can be realized in `ggplot2`. We will build on the knowledge you already acquired on the grammar of graphics, and we will see how the different components discussed in the previous chapter can be combined in order to get a more sophisticated and complex plot to represent your data.

Adding statistics

In the previous chapter, you saw how plots are composed of different components and how the data, aesthetic mapping, and geometry are the three minimally required elements needed in order to make a plot. In reality, statistics are also needed in order to draw a plot, but it is not necessarily needed to be specified since, as we have seen in the previous chapter, each geometry has default statistics, which, in many cases, are simply the identity statistics. This `stat` transformation actually does not produce anything on the data but leaves the data as it is in the plot. Another common stat that you have already used, probably without realizing it, is bin, which is used by default, for instance, in histograms and barplots, to divide the data into bins that are then represented in the graph.

The default stat used from each `geom` function will be sufficient in most common situations, but in some cases, it could be important for you to use a different stat or add an additional stat on top of the one used by default. In the following pages, we will see a few examples of two of the most important and commonly used statistics: smooth lines and regression lines.

Smooth lines

The smooth line implemented in `ggplot2` generates a local regression that will follow the data and allow you to have an idea of the fluctuation of the data points. The smooth line can be added in the plots in two different ways: using the `stat` function `stat_smooth()` or using the `geom` function `geom_smooth()`. Both these methods are very similar, and we will see some examples for both the methods in the following pages.

The `stat_smooth()` function is the statistic function responsible for creating the smooth line, so using this function will allow you to have greater statistical control over the computation of the smooth line. In this function, you have available the argument method, which allows you to choose the smoothing method used in the calculation. The options available are `lm`, `glm`, `gam`, `loess`, and `rlm`. As an alternative, a formula can also be specified in the formula argument. For a dataset with the number of observations smaller than 1,000, the default method is `loess`, while for data with more than 1,000 observations, the default is `gam`. The following is a summary table for the different methods, while for a detailed description of the statistical calculation used in each method, you can refer to the help page of the different functions:

Smoothing method	Package	Description
loess	stats	This fits a polynomial surface determined by one or more numerical predictors using local fitting. This is used by default when n<1000.
gam	mgcv	This fits a generalized additive model (gam) to the data. This is used by default when n>1000.
lm	stats	This fits a linear model.
rlm	MASS	This fits a linear model with a more robust fitting algorithm, which is less affected by outliers.

We will see a few examples of how to add a smooth line using the data from the `ToothGrowth` dataset that we have already used in the past chapters. In *Chapter 3, The Layers and Grammar of Graphics*, we have already seen how the `stat` function is simply added to the `geom` and the `ggplot()` functions to create facets with a smoother in each subplot using the following code:

```
ggplot(data=ToothGrowth, aes(x=dose, y=len, col=supp)) +
geom_point() + stat_smooth() + facet_grid(.~supp)
```

As you have seen in this example, we just added the specification of the `stat` transformation and the smooth line was added in each facet. This happens because the data and the aesthetic color are specified only in the main function, `ggplot()`, and for this reason, they are used for all the following functions. You have also probably noticed that when running the code, you see appearing on the screen a message specifying the method used in the calculation of the smooth line.

If we are not interested in having the data split into facets, we can simply remove the faceting argument. The following code shows this:

```
ggplot(data=ToothGrowth, aes(x=dose, y=len, col=supp)) +
geom_point() + stat_smooth()
```

The plot we just realized is represented in *Figure 4.1*. If you would like to use a different method to calculate the smoothing, you can specify it within the `stat_smooth()` function.

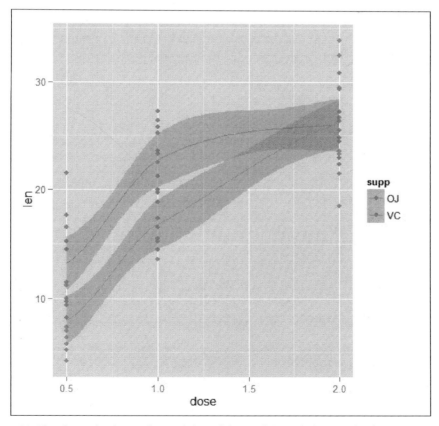

Figure 4.1: This shows the data and smooth line of the ToothGrowth dataset. The data is grouped by administration supplement

As you can see in the graph, without faceting, the data is in just one plot window but remains grouped by the administered supplement. Also, in this case, this depends on the fact that the data and the aesthetic attributes are specified only in the function creating the plot object. So, the same grouping based on the `supp` variable is applied to the `geom` attribute, which generates different colors, as well as the `stat` attribute, which generates two different smoothers. Keep in mind that if you want to get a different behavior, you can specify a different aesthetic mapping within the `stat_smooth()` function. For instance, let's assume that we want the data in the plot grouped by color depending on the `supp` variable, but we want a smooth line for the data altogether. We can specify independent aesthetic mapping within each function. The following code shows this:

```
ggplot() +
geom_point(data=ToothGrowth, aes(x=dose, y=len, col=supp)) +
stat_smooth(data=ToothGrowth, aes(x=dose, y=len))
```

As you can see in the resulting plot represented in *Figure 4.2*, we now have the data represented with the same grouping but with a smoothing that does not take into account the grouping. For this reason, the default color used in the new smoothing is different from the grouping colors.

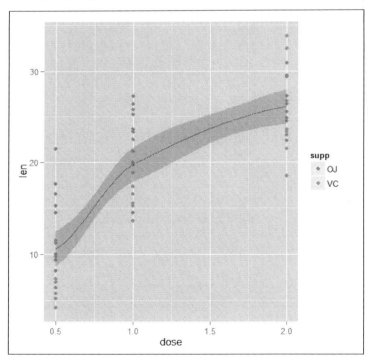

Figure 4.2: Here, the data and the smooth line of the ToothGrowth dataset are shown. The data is grouped by the administration of the supplement, while the smooth line is calculated on the overall dataset

Using the same approach, you can also combine several `stat` or `geom` functions by adding different degrees of representation of your data. In this case, it could be interesting to look at the same time at the smoothing lines specific to each subgroup of the supplement administration as well as the total tendency of the data, for instance, to see whether the overall tendency is driven particularly by one of the subgroups. The following code shows this:

```
ggplot() +
geom_point(data=ToothGrowth, aes(x=dose, y=len, col=supp)) +
stat_smooth(data=ToothGrowth, aes(x=dose, y=len)) +
stat_smooth(data=ToothGrowth, aes(x=dose, y=len,col=supp))
```

The resulting plot is shown in *Figure 4.3*:

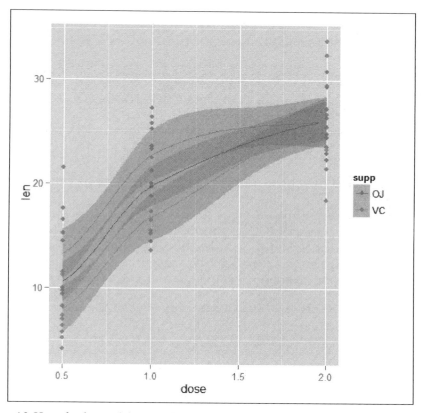

Figure 4.3: Here, the data and the smooth line of the ToothGrowth dataset are shown. The data is grouped by the administration of the supplement, and the smooth lines are calculated for each group as well as for the overall dataset

The `stat_smooth()` function contains two other arguments that can turn out to be very useful to adapt the data representation to your needs—the `se` and `span` arguments. The `se` argument is a logical argument, where you can specify whether or not you want the point-wise confidence interval, which is represented in gray, included in the plot the point-wise confidence interval, which is represented in gray. So, setting `se=FALSE`, you can switch off its representation. By default, the confidence interval is calculated at 95 percent; you can change that by changing the `level = 0.95` argument. The argument span controls the degree of smoothing of the line. With the smoothing, the fitting is calculated locally, so for a fit in a point x, the fitting is calculated using points in a neighbor of x. The span parameter defines the size of this neighbor. You can think of this option simply as a way to control the width of the smoothing. This parameter can be used when the `loess` smoothing method is used since it is passed directly to the `loess()` function of the `stats` package. If you want more details, you can look at the help page of this function. The default value, which was used in the previous examples, is 0.75.

The `stat_smooth()` function uses a specific default geometry, that is, `geom_smooth()`. As an alternative you can also use this function directly to generate the smooth line as you would use any other `geom` function. So, for instance, the following code would produce the same graph as in *Figure 4.1*:

```
ggplot(data=ToothGrowth, aes(x=dose, y=len, col=supp)) +
geom_smooth() + geom_point()
```

In a few cases, the use of the `geom_smooth()` function can be very useful. In fact, as we saw in the previous chapter, to realize a plot, you need to specify a geometry. This means that if you want smoothing of the data without representing the data, you can simply use the `geom_smooth()` function. As an alternative, you could use the `stat_smooth()` function and specify an empty `geom` function, such as `geom_blank()`. So, the following two blocks of code are equivalent, and they will produce a smoothing for each administration group without representing the observations:

```
ggplot(data=ToothGrowth, aes(x=dose, y=len, col=supp)) +
geom_smooth()


### Equivalent coding
ggplot(data=ToothGrowth, aes(x=dose, y=len, col=supp)) +
geom_blank()+stat_smooth()
```

You can see the resulting graph in *Figure 4.4*:

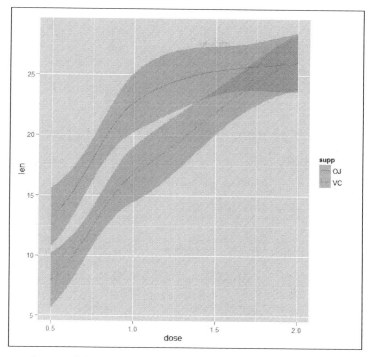

Figure 4.4: These are the smooth lines of the ToothGrowth dataset for each administration of the supplement

Linear regression

Linear regression can be used to represent as a straight line the relationship between a variable *x* and a variable *y*. As a difference from smoothing, in this case, the relationship is assumed to be linear and is calculated over the total range of the data available. As we have seen in the previous section, the `stat_smooth()` function allows us to select different methods, with one of them being the `lm` method, which calculates exactly the linear regression. Using the data from `ToothGrowth`, we can represent this time the linear regression of the data by representing a different regression line depending on the supplement administered. Here, you will see two examples of how to obtain the regression line and how to get the regression without the confidence interval represented on the plot:

```
## Regression with confidence interval
ggplot(data=ToothGrowth, aes(x=dose, y=len, col=supp)) +
geom_point()+stat_smooth(method="lm")


## Regression without confidence interval
```

```
ggplot(data=ToothGrowth, aes(x=dose, y=len, col=supp)) +
geom_point()+stat_smooth(method="lm", se=FALSE)
```

The resulting plots are represented in *Figure 4.5*:

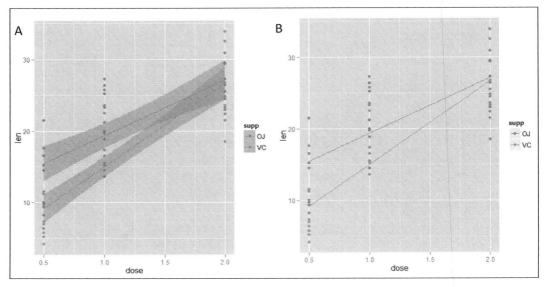

Figure 4.5: Here's the data and linear regression of the ToothGrowth dataset. (A) This shows linear regression with the confidence interval and (B) shows regression without the confidence interval

Statistics with faceting

We already introduced the basic concept of faceting in *Chapter 3, The Layers and Grammar of Graphics*, so now, we will see a few examples of how statistics can be used with faceting. Simply using the stat function with faceting, you will obtain smooth or linear regression in each facet calculated on the data of each facet, so, for instance, the following code will include a smooth line in each facet:

```
ggplot(data=ToothGrowth, aes(x=dose, y=len, col=supp)) +
geom_point() + stat_smooth() + facet_grid(.~supp)
```

The resulting graph is represented in *Figure 4.6*. As you have seen, we simply applied the `facet_grid()` function, together with the `stat_smooth()` function, and we were able to obtain a statistic description in each subset of data.

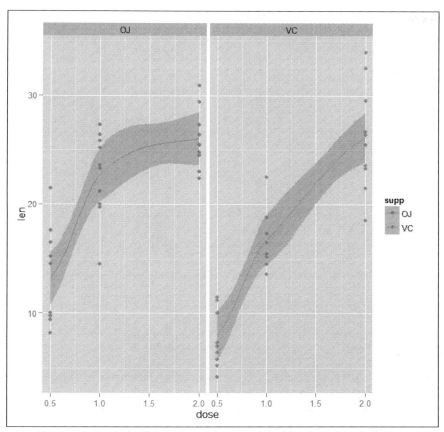

Figure 4.6: Here's the data and smooth regression of the ToothGrowth dataset with the data divided into facets

In some cases, on the other hand, you could be interested in visualizing different information. For instance, it could be interesting to get an overview of the tendency of the dataset together with the statistical description of each subgroup of the data. This kind of analysis can be done by adding the margin to the facets, which will add a column or row, along with the statistical analysis applied to them, to the facet containing all the data. This is how it would look for our example:.

```
ggplot(data=ToothGrowth, aes(x=dose, y=len, col=supp)) +
geom_point() + stat_smooth() + facet_grid(.~supp,margins=TRUE)
```

As you can see from the code, we used the `margin=TRUE` option to generate the additional facet with all the data. This kind of summary could be very useful if you are interested in comparing the overall smooth regression to one of each subgroup. The resulting plot is depicted in *Figure 4.7*:

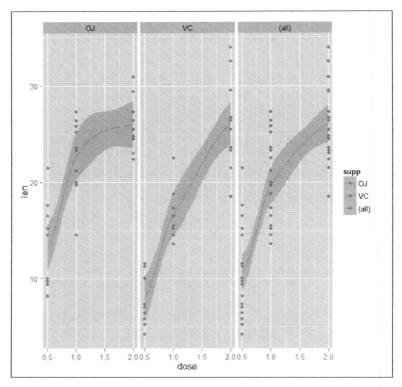

Figure 4.7: Here's the data and the smooth regression of the ToothGrowth dataset with the data divided into facets and also with a facet containing all the data

In other cases, you would want to apply the statistics only to one facet, for instance, if in some facets, you do not have enough data and you do not want to show any statistics since it would not be representative of the data group. You can do that by applying the statistical transformation to a subset of the data so that it will be applied only in the facet you are interested in. You can also use this approach if you want to apply different statistics to different facets. As an example, we will apply a smooth line to the first facet, corresponding to the data for the orange juice vehicle, and a linear regression, corresponding to the data for vitamin C, in the second facet:

```
ggplot(data=ToothGrowth, aes(x=dose, y=len, col=supp)) +
geom_point() + stat_smooth(data = subset(ToothGrowth, supp
=="OJ")) +
stat_smooth(data = subset(ToothGrowth, supp
```

```
=="VC"),method="lm") +
facet_grid(.~supp)
```

To make the code more clear, you can see each function on a different row. After creating the `ggplot` object and adding the observations as points, we apply the smooth statistic only on the subset of data where our `supp` variable is `OJ`. This means that only this data will have a smooth line, meaning only the first facet will have a smooth line. The same applies to the other facet except that this time we change the method used in the `stat_smooth()` function by selecting a linear method. You can see the resulting plot in *Figure 4.8*. The same approach can also be used to have the statistics only in one facet; in this case, you would simply apply the statistics to the facet you are interested in.

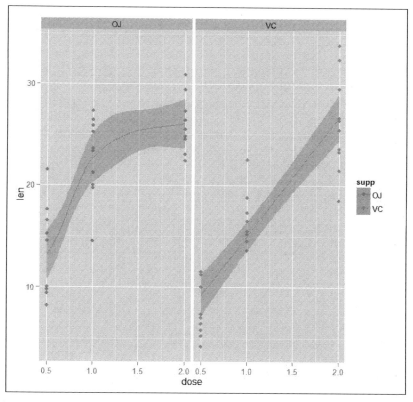

Figure 4.8: Shown here are the data and statistics regressions of the ToothGrowth dataset with the data divided into facets. The left facet contains the smooth line regression, while the right one is the linear regression

Advanced aesthetic mapping

In `ggplot2`, you have already seen how important the role played by aesthetic mapping is. You have the possibility of applying a very sophisticated and personalized scheme of aesthetic mapping in order to represent data or calculate statistical transformations based on the value of a variable used as a flagging factor. In the following sections, we will go through the different options of aesthetic mapping available and how they can be combined in your plot. For most of the examples, we will simply create small datasets by simulating random variables since, for the time being, we are just looking at the different mapping options for the data.

Typical aesthetic mappings available in ggplot2

You have already seen that the most relevant function used when applying aesthetic mapping is the `aes()` function. Leaving aside the mapping of the x and y variables, which were already covered in the previous chapter, we will now focus on the other mapping options. The most useful attributes to map are the color, the type of line, or the symbol used to represent the data (`linetype` or `shape` respectively, `size` of the symbols, and `transparency` (`alpha`). All these attributes can be mapped to different variables and combined in the plot in order to get the required data representation or the visual effect. In the examples we have come across until now, you have already seen some applications of the mapping for colors. The same approach can also be applied to the other attributes.

In the following example, we will create a dataset with three series of exponential values using exponents of 1, 1.5, and 2, and we will plot these three series of data. In the dataset, we will also include, together with our x and y values, a flag, which will allow us to retrieve the three different sequences of data, and we will use this flag to map the data. The following code shows this:

```
cont <-
data.frame(y=c(1:20,(1:20)^1.5,(1:20)^2),
x=1:20,group=rep(c(1,2,3),ea
ch=20))
```

We will represent the different sequences of data as points or lines using the `geom_point()` and `geom_line()` functions. The following code shows this:.

```
#### Data represented as points
ggplot(data=cont, aes(x=x, y=y, col=factor(group)))) + geom_point()

ggplot(data=cont, aes(x=x, y=y,
col=factor(group),size=factor(group))) +
geom_point()

ggplot(data=cont, aes(x=x, y=y,
col=factor(group),shape=factor(group))) +
geom_point()


#### Data represented as lines
ggplot(data=cont, aes(x=x, y=y, col=factor(group))) + geom_line()

ggplot(data=cont, aes(x=x, y=y,
col=factor(group),size=factor(group))) +
geom_line()

ggplot(data=cont, aes(x=x, y=y,
col=factor(group),linetype=factor(group))) +
geom_line()
```

As illustrated, we first assigned the grouping factor to the color attribute, we mapped the size of the line or points, and then we mapped the type of symbol used. In this last case, you would notice how we have used different arguments since point symbols can be mapped using the `shape` argument, while the tile of the line can be mapped with the `linetype` argument.

In *Chapter 3, The Layers and Grammar of Graphics*, you can find summary tables providing an overview of the aesthetics available for the most important `geom_x` functions, or as an alternative, you can also find this information on the help page of each function.

In *Figure 4.9*, you can see the plots we have obtained:

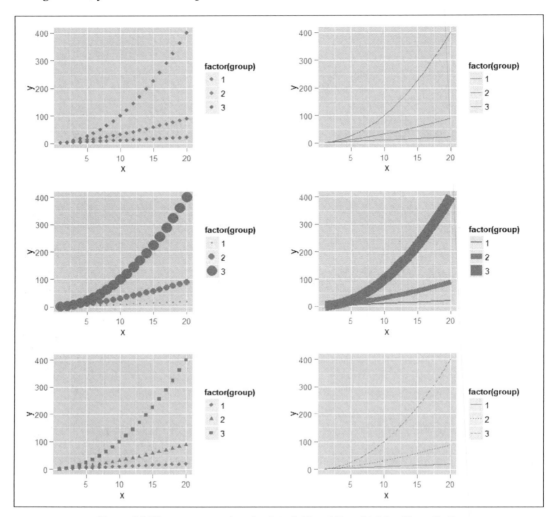

Figure 4.9: These are examples of points (left) and lines (right) with aesthetic mapping of colors (first row), size (second row), and type (third row)

You would also notice how, with the mapping size (second row of *Figure 4.9*), the aesthetic maps, by default, the size to the value of the mapping variable (group in our example). Consequently, group 3 has much bigger points and thicker lines compared to group 1.

In the next section, we will have a look at the mapping of the alpha parameter, which adds transparency to the element of the plot.

Mapping the aesthetic to new stat variables

In the previous chapter, we described how the `stat_x` functions work in general: they take the data you provide as input, and they use such data for statistical calculations. During such calculations, new variables can be created, such as the variable defining the bins or the variable defining the `count` element in a histogram. The output of these statistical transformations is also a dataset that contains the original data and the new variables created in the process, and that depends on the specific `stat_x` function used. In *Chapter 3, The Layers and Grammar of Graphics,* you can find a summary table for these `stat` functions that also contains specific new variables created for the most important functions. These newly created variables are quite interesting since they can also be used in the plot that contains the `stat_x` function. This is exactly how the results of the statistical transformations are represented in the plot. On top of this default representation, you can also use these newly created variables to represent additional information on the plot, or you can, for instance, map aesthetic attributes to such variables.

We will now just see a simple example showing how we can use such variables which, in some cases, can produce a very nice effect on the histogram, for instance. We will just create a simple normal distribution with default values (0 as the mean and 1 as the standard deviation) using the `rnorm` function, and then we will create a histogram of such a distribution. We can then map the filling color to the number of observations in each `bin` available in the new `count` variable created by the `stat_bin()` function. Just remember that, in order to avoid errors because of variables with the same name in the original dataset, the newly created variables must be surrounded by `..`, so in our example, we would need to use `..count..`. The following code shows this:

```
set.seed(1234)
x <-data.frame(x=rnorm(1000))
ggplot(data=x, aes(x=x, fill=..count..)) + geom_histogram()
```

Since we are performing a simulation of random numbers, as the first thing, we set up the `seed` function used in the random number generation process so that we get the same results every time we run the code. The plot we just obtained is represented in *Figure 4.10*. As illustrated, the use of such variables is quite similar to the traditional variable; the trickiest part is to know which additional variables you have available for the statistic you are using, and for this, you can use the tables in the previous chapter. With them, you can also get new ideas about new applications that better fit your needs.

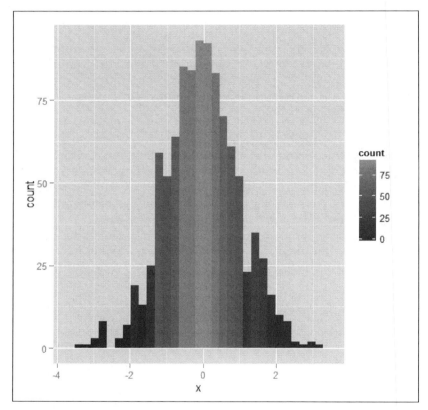

Figure 4.10: Here's a histogram of a normally distributed random variable representing the data count (default option) with the color intensity proportional to the data count

Applying this method to aesthetic mapping, we use a continuous scale of color tones to map the observation count. Since the scale is continuous, we cannot apply this method on geometries with only one continuous plot area, such as `geom_density()`, which generate a smooth estimate of the kernel density. We have used this function in some of the examples in *Chapter 2, Getting Started*.

On the other side, you can apply it to the histogram representing the density of observations. We can, in fact, use the new variable density created by the `stat_bin()` function to represent as a *y* value the density of observations present in each bin and at the same time use a filling color proportional to the observations. The following code shows this:

```
ggplot(data=x, aes(x=x)) +
geom_histogram(aes(y=..density..,fill=..density..))
```

We can also combine multiple geometries on the same plot and also add the kernel density function on top of the histogram we have obtained. The following code shows this:

```
ggplot(data=x, aes(x=x)) +
geom_histogram(aes(y=..density..,fill=..density..)) +
geom_density()
```

You can see both plots in *Figure 4.11*. You can see how the data density is scaled to integrate to 1 and how in this case we have used the new variable `..density..` not only for the color filling aesthetic, but also for the plotting value *y*. In the previous example, when representing the data count, we did not need to specify the *y* variable since the default behavior of `geom_histogram()` is to represent the data count.

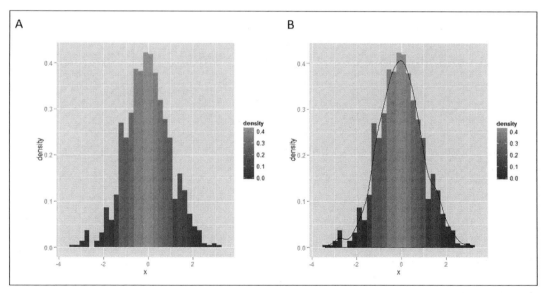

Figure 4.11: (A) This is a histogram of a normally distributed random variable representing data density with color intensity proportional to the data density scaled to 1. (B) This is the same plot as (A) but also includes the estimate for the kernel density function

As you can see from the plot in *Figure 4.11*, the graphical effect that we have produced with this mapping is to have the data bins represented with a color shade that is proportional to the amount of data in each bin. A similar effect can be obtained by assigning a mapping to the alpha variable, which defines the transparency of the data. We have already used the alpha attributes in some other examples previously, but in this case, we will use it for an actual aesthetic mapping instead of assigning a fixed value to it. This means that we will need to give the definition of alpha in the aes() function, together with the other aesthetic attributes. The following code shows this:

```
ggplot(data=x, aes(x=x)) + geom_histogram(aes(alpha=..count..))
```

As illustrated in the resulting plot in *Figure 4.12 (A)*, the default behavior of alpha mapping is to use gray scales since it is not a mapping of colors but rather a mapping of transparency. It is also possible to combine the mapping of the previous example with the filling, together with the transparency, and you can see the resulting plot in *Figure 4.12 (B)*. The following code shows this:

```
ggplot(data=x, aes(x=x)) +
geom_histogram(aes(alpha=..count..,fill=..count..))
```

As is apparent, the effect is quite redundant since both mappings produce a similar effect although one is based on color and the other on transparency. You would also notice how the two mappings are considered independent and ggplot2 will produce two different scales for them.

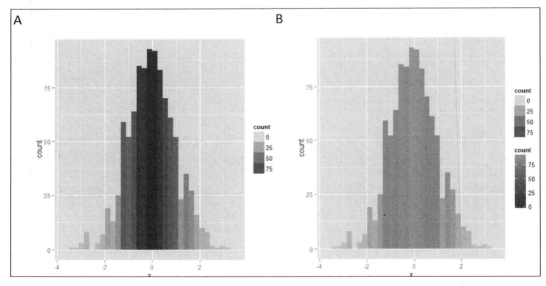

Figure 4.12: (A) This is a histogram of a normally distributed random variable representing the data count with transparency (alpha) mapped to the data count. (B) This is the same plot as (A) but also includes a filling mapping to the data count

If you want to try out such a mapping on real data, you can go to *Chapter 2, Getting Started*, where we used the `iris` dataset as an example for histograms and density plots. You could, for instance, add `alpha` mapping to *Figure 2.4* of *Chapter 2, Getting Started*, with the following code:

```
ggplot(data=iris,
aes(x=Petal.Length,col=Species,fill=Species,alpha=..count..)) +
geom_histogram()
```

Difference in mapping continuous and categorical variables

In the preceding chapter, in *Figure 3.4*, we saw an overview of a few options of scales and the difference in scales between continuous and categorical variables. In this section, we will have a closer look at how the assignment of scales is done using these different scales and at how you can control this aspect to get a grip on the scale that is used.

Let's first create a small dataset with four different distributions of random variables:

```
dist <- data.frame(value=rnorm(10000, 1:4), group=1:4)
```

The distributions we just created are all normal with a standard deviation of 1 but are built around an increasing mean, so the first distribution will have 1 as the mean, the second will have 2 as the mean, and so on.

We can plot such data as jittered points using a different color for each group; with the following code, we obtain the plot in *Figure 4.13*:

```
ggplot(dist, aes(x=group, y=value, color=group)) +
geom_jitter(alpha=0.5)
```

As illustrated, we simply represented the values of the distributions on the *y* axis for the different groups that are on the *x* axis. As shown, the default scale selected by `ggplot2` is a continuous scale where the color intensity is associated with the color value. Of course, this is not what we are interested in since we just wanted to represent the different distributions with a different color that is easy to identify and not connected in a color scale. The reason for this is related to the type of values that we represented.

In fact, in our dataset, the variables contained in the `group` column are numeric, and this means that `ggplot2` will treat them as connected in a numeric scale and consequently will associate with them a continuous scale. One way to overcome this issue is to simply change the variable to `factor`. In this way, the numbers will be treated only as levels and not as numeric values.

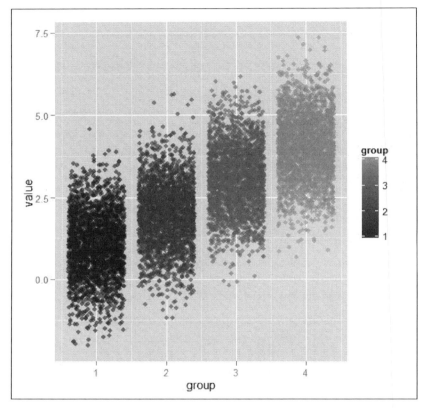

Figure 4.13: This is a representation of different distributions with jittered points

This can be done, of course, directly in the dataset in simple examples as ours, but in most cases, where, eventually, you will use a big dataset, you would not want to change its variables for each plot. In this situation, it is much more convenient to change the variables directly in the plot. The following is the code to have the grouping variable as a factor:

```
ggplot(dist, aes(x=group, y=value,
color=as.factor(group))) +
geom_jitter(alpha=0.5)
```

In *Figure 4.14*, you can see the resulting plot. As illustrated, changing the variable to `factor` will produce a default plot with the `as.factor(group)` scale notation. This can be changed by changing the title of the legend; we will see how to do that in the next chapter. The use of converting a variable from `numeric` to `factor` can turn out to be very handy, and I am sure that you will find this approach when browsing for help. In the following code, you can find an example of such an approach on a real dataset—the `mtcars` dataset. In this case, the grouping variable, that is, the number of cylinders of the cars, is also treated as numeric, but the idea is, of course, to simply use this variable as a grouping variable. The following code shows this:

```
ggplot(mtcars, aes(mpg, wt)) + geom_point(aes(color = cyl))
ggplot(mtcars, aes(mpg, wt)) + geom_point(aes(color = factor(cyl)))
```

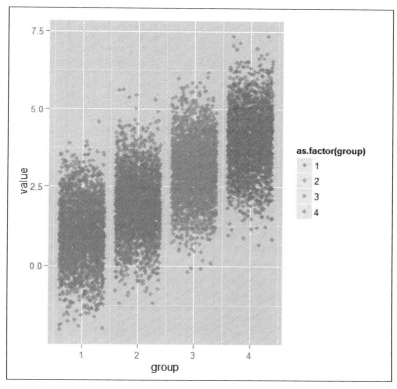

Figure 4.14: This is a representation of the different distributions with jittered points and with the grouping variable treated as a factor

Adding text and reference lines to plots

In this section, we will take a look at some of the most useful annotations you would want to add to a plot. After you have represented your data, you would probably need to add a specific reference to the plot, for instance, vertical bars, text, or other types of annotations. The ggplot2 package provides a vast variety of options, and for a complete reference, you can have a look at the ggplot2 documentation website http://docs.ggplot2.org. In this section, we will take a look at the most important annotations.

Let's consider again our dataset that we created previously just by generating a series of normally distributed random numbers.

```
x <- data.frame(x=rnorm(1000))
```

We can, for instance, represent this distribution using a histogram. In this case, it could be useful to add a vertical bar to the plot representing the mean of the distribution. As for graphics, ggplot2 also provides three major functions to produce such reference lines:

- geom_hline() for horizontal lines
- geom_vline() for vertical lines
- geom_abline() using which any line can be created by specifying the slope and intercept

The first two functions are a special case of this last one since they allow you only to represent lines parallel to the axis. In the following code, we use the relative function to add a vertical line to the histogram corresponding to the median of the distribution:

```
ggplot(x, aes(x=x)) +
geom_histogram(alpha=0.5) +
geom_vline(aes(xintercept=median(x)),

color="red", linetype="dashed", size=1)
```

We also specified the color, the type of line, and the size the line should have. You can see how such arguments are similar to the arguments used by other graphical packages in R. As you have seen in this case, we specified the intercept on the *x* axis by calculating it from our data. This is a very useful approach since even if you changed the data, the plot would still be produced correctly. Of course, as an alternative, we could also specify the numeric value at which we want to have our intercept. For instance, we can add to our plot a horizontal line corresponding to a level of 50 in our data count. In this case, we will draw a solid black line:

```
ggplot(x, aes(x=x)) +
geom_histogram(alpha=0.5) +
geom_vline(aes(xintercept=median(x)), color="red", linetype="dashed",
size=1) +
geom_hline(aes(yintercept=50), col="black", linetype="solid")
```

You can see the resulting plot in *Figure 4.15*:

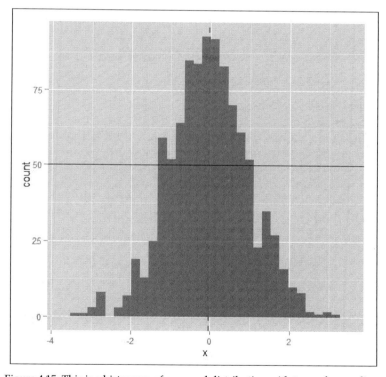

Figure 4.15: This is a histogram of a normal distribution with two reference lines

Together with the vertical line, it is also possible to add text to the plot as an annotation. Text as well as lines can also be mapped to variables, producing a plot representing text corresponding to the variables, for instance. In this case, it would be nice to include in the plot an indication that the red vertical bar refers to the median and specify its numeric value. We can do that using the `geom_text()` function, in which we can specify the text we want to add as well as its coordinates. The following code shows this:

```
ggplot(x, aes(x=x)) +

geom_histogram(alpha=0.5) +
geom_vline(aes(xintercept=median(x)), color="red", linetype="dashed",

size=1) +
geom_hline(aes(yintercept=50), col="black", linetype="solid") +
geom_text(aes(x=median(x),y=80),label="Median",hjust=1) +
geom_text(aes(x=median(x),y=80,label=round(median(x),

digit=3)),hjust=-0.5)
```

Within the `geom_text()` function, we also used aesthetic mapping to define the position of the objects. As you can see, we had the possibility of using a numeric value as we did for the y argument, as well as a calculated value as we did for the x value, which is calculated using the `median()` function. In this situation, when you actually don't know the value but you calculate it within the plot function, it is very useful to use adjustment arguments to add an offset to the text so that it does not overlap with the median line. You can do that using `hjust` for horizontal adjustment and `vjust` for the vertical ones. These adjustments will represent the text with a shift from its original position equivalent to the value that you provided. In our example, the word `"Median"` will be shifted by 1 unit to the left, while the numeric value of the median will be shifted by 0.5 to the right since the value is negative. Since the default of the digits produces a number with too high a level of precision, you would often need to round off these calculated values, and that's what we did using the `round()` function, in which we specified the number of digits to represent.

Finally, `ggplot2` also provides an `annotate()` function that allows you to easily create annotations to the plot. You can use it to add specific lines, text, and a shading area to the plot by providing the limits on the axes. You would find an idea of the possible annotation by looking at the help page of the function or on the `ggplot2` website. Additional examples are also shown on the `ggplot2` website under the `theme()` function. In this case, we will have a look at one example. We will draw a shade area on our histogram covering the interquartile range between the twenty-fifth and the seventy-fifth percentiles.

The following code shows this:

```
ggplot(x, aes(x=x)) +
geom_histogram(alpha=0.5) +
geom_vline(aes(xintercept=median(x)), color="red",linetype="dashed",
size=1) +
geom_hline(aes(yintercept=50), col="black",linetype="solid") +
geom_text(aes(x=median(x),y=80),label="Median",hjust=1) + geom_text(aes(x
=median(x),y=80,label=round(median(x)
, digit=3)),hjust=-0.5) +
annotate("rect", xmin = quantile(x$x, probs = 0.25), xmax = quantile(x$x,
probs = 0.75), ymin = 0, ymax = 100,
alpha = .2, fill="blue")
```

As illustrated, in the `annotate()` function, we selected the type of geometry we want to represent, that is, the rectangular one, and then we defined the extremes of the area. You would also notice that since, in this case, we are not mapping aesthetics, for our calculations, we need to provide a specific reference to the dataset, for instance, in `quantile(x$x, probs = 0.75)`, we need to specify the actual column in the datasets. On the other hand, for the calculation of the median, within the `aes()` function, we were able to specify only the column in the dataset since the data was already loaded in the plot object ready for aesthetic mapping. You can see the final plot with all our annotations in *Figure 4.16*:

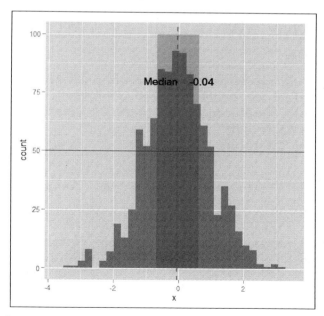

Figure 4.16: This is a histogram of a normal distribution with two reference lines, the notation for the median value, and a shade area for the interquartile range

The `annotate()` function can be very useful to quickly make annotations without having the data in a data frame structure, for instance, in this case, we were able to draw a rectangular area without the need to have to use `geom` functions.

Add text and reference lines with facets

In the examples we just discussed, we applied text and reference lines to only one plot, but in many cases, you would probably have plots divided into facets in which you would also like to add reference lines. One easy way to do that is using the same approach we discussed in the *Adding statistics* section at the beginning of this chapter. We can add text as well as the reference lines by applying the layer to only a subset of data. We can see an example of this using the `dist` dataset, which we created in the previous sections, and which contains four different normal distributions. We will represent such distributions in facets, and we will apply a reference line on the median value of the first distribution as well as its numeric value. The following code shows this:

```
ggplot(dist, aes(x=value, fill=as.factor(group))) +
geom_histogram(alpha=0.5) +
geom_vline(data = subset(dist, group
=="1"), aes(xintercept=median(value)), color="black",
linetype="dashed", size=1) +
geom_text(data = subset(dist, group
=="1"),aes(x=median(value),y=350,label=round(median(value),
digit=3)),hjust=-0.2) +
facet_grid(.~group)
```

As you can see from the preceding code, we simply applied the text and the vertical line only to the data with the `group` value equal to 1. This way, we add these elements only to the first facet. You can see the resulting graph in *Figure 4.17*. You would also notice how selecting the data within the `geom_text()` and `geom_vline()` functions, the median is only calculated on this subset of data.

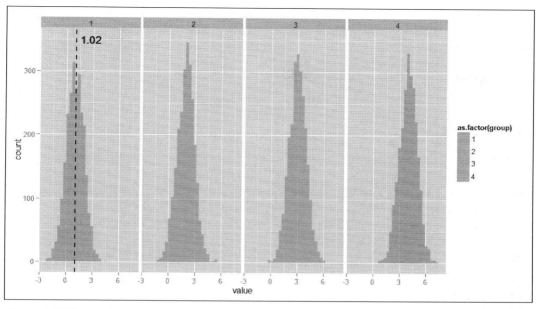

Figure 4.17: This is a histogram of the dist dataset with a facet for each distribution. A reference line indicating the median is added on the first facet and the median value is also included

Using the same approach, you can add the median reference line and the median value to the other facets; you will just need to also include the code for the other groups as well. On the other hand, you will get reference lines on the plots that will not match the colors used in the distributions since we include a component after the other instead of letting ggplot2 split the data and make the color assignments. To solve this, recall the default assignments of colors and then use them in the plot. We already mentioned in *Chapter 3*, *The Layers and Grammar of Graphics*, how equally spaced colors on the color wheel are assigned the default to categorical variables. Here, we will show a practical example of that.

First of all, we create a vector with the first four default colors assigned by ggplot2 to categorical variables. The following code shows this:

```
myColours <- scales::hue_pal()(4)
```

The myColours vector will contain the four colors in the same order as assigned by ggplot2, so the first will be assigned to the first variable, the second to the second one, and so on.

We will then create the plot using the same method used before with the difference that the colors used to draw the vertical line will be taken from this vector of colors. Since this code is quite long, you have the different parts of the code divided by a comment indicating to which facet it applies. You can also see italicized the code for the first facet since the remaining code will have a similar structure for the other facets. The following code shows this:

```
ggplot(dist, aes(x=value, fill=as.factor(group))) +

geom_histogram(alpha=0.5)+

### Facet 1

geom_vline(data = subset(dist, group ==1),
aes(xintercept=median(value)), color=myColours[1], linetype="dashed",
size=1.5)+geom_text(data = subset(dist, group
==1),aes(x=median(value),y=350,label=round(median(value),
digit=3)),hjust=-0.2)+

### Facet 2

geom_vline(data = subset(dist, group==2),
aes(xintercept=median(value)), color=myColours[2], linetype="dashed",
size=1.5)+

geom_text(data = subset(dist, group
==2),aes(x=median(value),y=350,label=round(median(value),
digit=3)),hjust=-0.2)+

### Facet 3

geom_vline(data = subset(dist, group==3),
aes(xintercept=median(value)), color=myColours[3], linetype="dashed",
size=1.5)+geom_text(data = subset(dist, group
==3),aes(x=median(value),y=350,label=round(median(value),
digit=3)),hjust=-0.2)+

### Facet 4

geom_vline(data = subset(dist, group==4),
aes(xintercept=median(value)), color=myColours[4], linetype="dashed",
size=1.5)+geom_text(data = subset(dist, group
==4),aes(x=median(value),y=350,label=round(median(value),
digit=3)),hjust=-0.2)+facet_grid(.~group)
```

The resulting plot is represented in *Figure 4.18*. As you have seen, we now have the vertical reference lines with a matching color that is the same as the one used to fill the histograms, with a resulting nicer graphical effect. When using this approach, you just need to be sure that the reference lines can be clearly distinguished since you are drawing them on top of histograms having the same color. A possible solution, used in our example, is to slightly increase the size of the lines. In the final plot, you can also see how in each facet we obtain the same median calculation that was used to simulate the original distributions. Clearly, you could use the same method even to the text added to the facet by specifying the color in the geom_text() function.

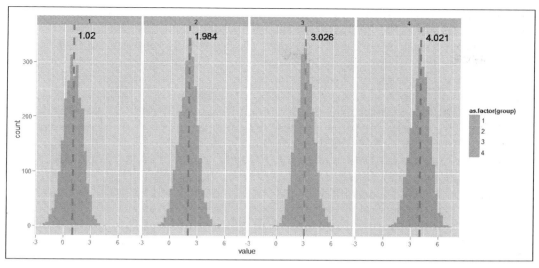

Figure 4.18: This is a histogram of the dist dataset with a facet for each distribution. A reference line indicating the median is added in each facet with a color matching the ggplot default assignment

Plots with polar coordinates

In this section, we will have a look at a few plots that can be created using polar coordinates. We have already introduced this coordinate system in the previous chapter. Just remember that you should always use these coordinates with caution since the representation of data in circular form can generate very pronounced perceptual problems concerning the relative areas in the plot.

The most important plots that you can realize with these coordinates are the pie chart, the bullseye chart, and the coxcomb diagram. For our examples, we will use the `movie` dataset, which we created in previous chapters and the `myMovieData` dataset, and we will represent in these different plots the proportions of movies within each category.

A pie chart

A pie chart in `ggplot2` corresponds to a stacked bar chart in polar coordinates. This means that to produce a pie chart, we will first create a bar chart with bars stacked one on top of the other, and then we will change the coordinate system. The following code shows this:

```
ggplot(data=myMovieData,
aes(x=factor(1),fill=factor(Type))) +
geom_bar(width = 1) + coord_polar(theta = "y")
```

This code can turn out to be quite tricky to follow, but with more details, it should become much clearer. The first two lines simply define a bar with the count for each movie type stacked on top of each other along the y axis, with the `type` variable defining the filling color. This variable is finally the one that we will end up representing in the pie chart. The definition of `x=factor(1)` doesn't do anything, and it can contain any value; its scope is simply to have just one factor that will be the x axis of our hypothetical bar chart. The `width=1` parameter basically defines the radius of our pie chart. Any value greater than 1 will not produce any change since 1 means that the bars of our plot will cover the whole plot area. On the other hand, a value lower than 1 would produce a tighter bar. Finally, with the last line, we just make polar the coordinate y, which is the axis along which we have built our bar chart. In *Figure 4.19* are represented the bar plots and the resulting pie charts obtained when changing the coordinates to polar for `width=1` and for `width=0.5`. As you can see, even using a smaller width value can create a nice pie chart effect with an empty area in the middle.

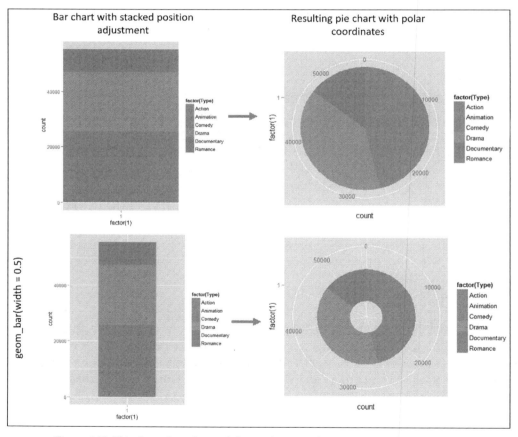

Figure 4.19: This shows bar plots and the resulting pie charts obtained when changing the coordinates to polar for width=1 and for width=0.5

A bullseye chart

A bullseye chart is a chart in which the variables are represented in a circular way with an area proportional to the variable value. The difference compared with the pie chart is that the variables are represented in a concentric way, as in the center of a target ("bull's-eye"). In ggplot2, these plots are realized by producing a bar chart as shown in *Figure 4.19*, but instead of stretching the *y* axis along the polar coordinates, in this case, we simply stretch them along the *x* axis. The following code shows how this is done:

```
ggplot(data=myMovieData, aes(x=factor(1),fill=factor(Type))) +
geom_bar(width = 1) + coord_polar()
```

The resulting plot is represented in *Figure 4.20*:

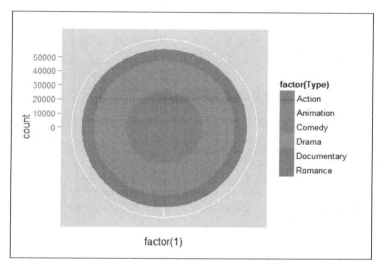

Figure 4.20: This is an example of a bullseye chart realized with the myMovieData dataset

A coxcomb diagram

The coxcomb diagram is similar to a pie chart, but the areas representing the data in the pie are not normalized to cover the whole area of the circle. They can be realized in a similar way to the pie chart by producing a normal bar chart and converting its coordinates into polar coordinates. In this case, the bar chart is not realized with the stacked position adjustment, but the data is placed such that one piece of data is next to another along the *x* axis of our bar chart. The following code shows this:

```
ggplot(data=myMovieData,

aes(x=Type,fill=factor(Type))) +
geom_bar(width = 1) + coord_polar(theta = "x")
```

You can then see the resulting chart in *Figure 4.21*:

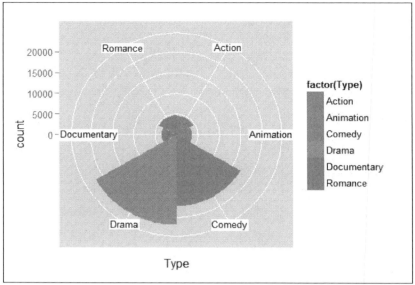

Figure 4.21: Here's an example of a coxcomb diagram realized with the myMovieData dataset

Further reading

Additional examples can be found on the respective help pages of each function mentioned or on the package webpage at http://docs.ggplot2.org/.

Summary

In this chapter, we had a look at a few examples of more advanced plots that can be realized with ggplot2. We went through the inclusion of statistics in the plot by showing examples for the smooth and linear regression. We then covered examples of more complex mapping of aesthetic variables, for instance, by recalling the variables that are created from the statistical transformations and how to use them to create histograms with shades of colors that are related to the count or density of the data. We then also saw a few examples of how annotations can be added to plots. Finally, we saw a few examples of how to realize a polar area chart using the polar coordinates. In the next chapter, we will look at how to control plot detail using ggplot2 and explore axis scales, legends, and themes in detail.

5
Controlling Plot Details

Although, by now, you have gained a good understanding of how to make plots, you certainly realize that we did not discuss how to change the default details of the plot, which are automatically set up by ggplot2. In this chapter, we will go through how to personalize details such as the plot title and axis, axis scales, plot background, and the legend details. We will then see examples of of layout changes that can be applied to facet plots.

Exploring scales

We already discussed scales in different situations but, in this case, we will focus on certain general aspects that will turn out to be essential for you to understand how to fully utilize the different scales available. Generally speaking, the scales are assigned during the aesthetic mapping and are then used to define guides to trace from the represented objects back to the data by creating legends as well as the plot axis. You can add a scale to your plot or modify the default values of the scale using one of the scale functions. These functions have the general structure of scale_aesthetic_scale, where aesthetic represents the aesthetic on which the scale is applied and scale represents the name of the scale on which it is used. Typical aesthetic values can be, for instance, color, x, y, fill, shape, or size, while examples of scales are hue, brewer, gradient, and log10. So, for instance, the scale_color_gradient() function defines the gradient of colors. Take for example a case where different shades of a certain color are used to map data, as we did in *Figure 5.1*. Another example is scale_color_hue(), which is used for equally spaced colors, for instance, for mapping categorical values to the color aesthetic, while scale_fill_hue() is the corresponding scale for the fill aesthetic. You also have the option to define your own scale for discrete data using the scale_manual() function. Also, keep in mind that if you want to set one of the aesthetics to a certain value, you need to use the I() operator, so to use only the color red, you can use the code color=I("red") as we already described in *Chapter 2, Getting Started*.

In this chapter, we will see several examples of scales and their use, but we will not go into all the details as we shall see from our examples that in many cases their usage is almost the same. If you want an overview of the different scales available, you can have a look at them on the `ggplot2` website documentation at `http://docs.ggplot2.org`.

Grayscale plots for black-and-white publications

In some cases, you may need to produce plots using only black-and-white colors. You can convert your plot to grayscale simply using the `scale_color_grey()` and `scale_fill_grey()` functions depending on the aesthetic. For instance, the scatterplot from the previous chapter can be rendered in grayscale with the following command:

```
myScatter + scale_color_grey()
```

The plot title and axis labels

As you saw when creating a plot with `ggplot2`, the default result will be a plot without any title and with axis labels corresponding to the names of the variables represented in the plot. In many cases, you will want to personalize things such as labels, particularly if you are interested in including not only the name of the variable, but also its units. Alternatively, you might also be interested in providing more descriptive labels than simply the title of the variable. In this section, we will see examples of how to change three different types of details: how to change the title and labels of the axis, how to change the scale represented in the *x* and *y* axes, and how to remove them if you don't want to have them in the plot.

In order to change the plot title, there are two main options that you can choose from:

- There is the possibility of changing the title and axis label using specific functions: `ggtitle()` for the title and `xlab()` and `ylab()` for the axes
- Alternatively, you can use the `labs()` function in which you can specify both the axis and the title using the argument titles, x and y

As a simple example, let's take the histogram we created in the previous chapter with the following command:

```
set.seed(1234)

x <- data.frame(x=rnorm(1000))

ggplot(data=x, aes(x=x, fill=..count..)) + geom_histogram()
```

As illustrated in *Figure 4.9,* the default plot obtained has the name of the variable used on the *x* axis, which, in this case, is *x*, and on the *y* axis the plot has the name of the variable count, which is created by the `stat` function. We can, additionally, change the plot title and labels of the axis as mentioned before. Here, you have an example of how that can be done using a unique call to `labs()` or by modifying independently; you can choose what is more convenient to you since there is no difference in the result. The following command shows this:

```
###### Using labs()
ggplot(data=x, aes(x=x, fill=..count..)) + geom_histogram() +
labs(title="This is my histogram", x="Random variable", y="Number
of times")


#### Using the individual functions
ggplot(data=x, aes(x=x, fill=..count..)) + geom_histogram() +
ggtitle("This is my histogram") + xlab("Random variable") +
ylab("Number of times")
```

Both commands generate the plot presented in *Figure 5.1.* When using the `labs()` function, you can also specify only some of the arguments, so you can also use that function to add the title without changing the labels, for instance.

Split long titles into more lines

Sometimes, you may want to include in the plot a longer title or additional explanation. In this situation, you may end up with text that is too long to be included in the upper part of the graph. You can break a title into multiple lines using the special character \n, which indicates that you are going to a new line in many programming languages. This can turn out to be quite useful if you want to keep a longer title centered in the picture. You can include this special character directly in the text, so the title of our previous example would be as follows:

```
labs(title="This is \n my histogram", x="Random
variable", y="Number of times")
```

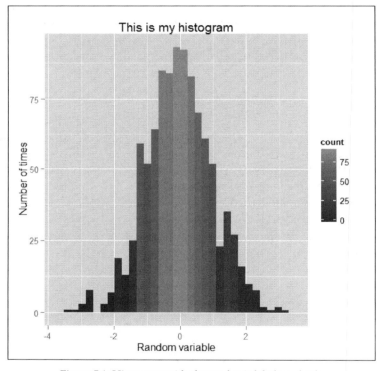

Figure 5.1: Histogram with changed axis labels and title

Axis scales

Together with axis labels, you will also often need to change the axis scales. For instance, you may want to change the scale in log values or modify the default range values included in the axis when creating the plot. In this section, we will take a look at exactly how to do these modifications. The axis scales as well as the legends are derived from the scales used in aesthetic mappings, so, in many cases, if you want to manipulate such values, you will need to use the scale function relative to your specific situation. For this reason, we will treat the plots with only discrete scales as different from those with only continuous scales.

The discrete axis

You may have a plot with discrete scales, for instance, when you represent data grouped in categories along one of the axes. As an example, we will use the dataset with the four different normal distributions that we created in the previous chapter with the next command. In this case, we will just directly define the grouping variable as a factor so that we don't need to convert numbers to factors later on. The following command shows this:

```
dist <- data.frame(value=rnorm(10000, 1:4), group=factor(1:4))
```

Our `dist` dataset will contain four different normal distributions, and we will visualize them as boxplots with the different groups defined by the variable group along the *x* axis, as follows:

```
myBoxplot <- ggplot(dist, aes(x=group, y=value, fill=group)) +
geom_boxplot()
```

The resulting plot is represented in *Figure 5.2(A)*. In this case, we have an *x* axis composed of discrete data, so if we, for instance, want to change the order of such data, we can do that using the scale function for discrete data and apply it to the *x* axis aesthetic. We will then use the `scale_x_discrete()` function. In the upcoming examples, we will consider scale transformations to the *x* axis, but the same transformation can be applied to the *y* axis by replacing *x* with *y* in the function or argument names. The following command shows this:

```
myBoxplot + scale_x_discrete(limits=c("1","3","2","4"))
```

As illustrated in *Figure 5.2(B)*, we have changed the order of the data to the order we have specified.

Reversing the order of discrete variables

We have seen how to manually set the order of discrete variables. You can also use this approach to invert the order of the variables, but, in case you are working on a dataset with many levels in the grouping variable, it may be handy to use the rev() function. This basic R function simply inverts the order of its elements, so using it in the limits argument will make the command shorter and easier to read. The following command shows how you can apply this method to invert the order of your variables; just remember that you need to specify the dataset explicitly since, in this case, you are actually using the vector of levels of your grouping variable directly:

```
myBoxplot + scale_x_discrete(limits =
rev(levels(dist$group)))
```

In our previous examples, we specified the order of the discrete variables using the limits argument of the scale function. There are also other arguments that you can use in this function to change default values in the scale. These arguments will be very similar to other scale functions, so we will not list them for all scale functions we will mention in the next pages. You can always check them in the help page of the specific function you are interested in. For the scale_x_discrete() function, the common available arguments are the following:

- name: This defines the name of the scale and so the label of the axis. Aesthetics that are used in the legend define the name of the legend.

- breaks: This controls the breaks in the guide and so which values appear on the axis or legend. The value is NULL for no breaks.

- labels: This defines the labels that should appear on the breakpoints defined by breaks; the value is NULL for no labels.

- na.value: This is how missing values should be displayed, for instance, by providing the value that should be represented as replacement.

- limits: This defines the limits of the data range and the default order of how they are displayed.

- guide: This is used to control the legend.

In most cases, the arguments of the specific scale functions are passed to a more general function, which then actually constructs the scale. For this reason, you will not find a description of such arguments on the help page of the scale function but on the help page of the constructor function. On the help page of the scale function, you will find specified which scale constructor is used. In our previous examples, for instance, the scale_x_discrete() as well as scale_y_discrete() scale functions use the discrete_scale() scale constructor.

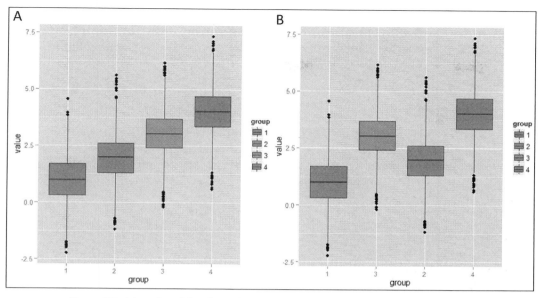

Figure 5.2: A boxplot of distributions in the dataset dist with default settings (A) and with the changed order of the discrete variable on the x axis (B)

The continuous axis

When dealing with continuous scales, two very common adjustments on the scale you will probably need to make in some cases are modifying the default data range represented in the plot and inversing the direction of the data. As we have seen in the previous section, the scale functions provided the `limits` argument, which allowed us to set the limits of the axis. We can, for instance, change the limits of the *y* axis in the boxplot we just created by extending it from -10 to 10, as shown in the following command:

```
myBoxplot + scale_y_continuous(limits=c(-10,10))
```

As an alternative, you can also use the `xlim` and `ylim` functions if you only need to change the range, so, for instance, the following command will produce the same result:

```
myBoxplot + ylim(-10,10)
```

The resulting plot is shown in *Figure 5.3(A)*.

If you want to make sure that a value in the range is included in your plot, you can also use the `expand_limits()` function. This function will increase the range plotted, making sure that all the values within the specified limits are included. For instance, if we want to make sure that the value -10 is represented in our plot, we can use this function, the resulting plot of which is represented in *Figure 5.3(B)*:

```
myBoxplot + expand_limits(y=-10)
```

This function can be very handy since you only specify the values that should be included, so if you change the data in you plot or reuse part of your code, the limits are also be applied to the new plot. On the other hand, just keep in mind that the `expand_limits()` function cannot be used to shrink the range represented. Take the following command as an example:

```
myBoxplot + expand_limits(y=0)
```

The preceding command will not produce any change in our original plot since 0 is already included in the range plotted.

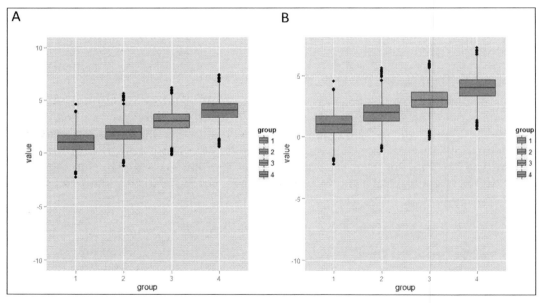

Figure 5.3: A boxplot of distributions in the dataset dist with the y axis range from -10 to 10 (A) and the expanded range to include value the value -10 (B)

Axis transformations

By default, scales in plots are linear, but you have the option to replace this with a transformed scale for your axis. This can be done in several different ways, but the two main options are to transform the axis by changing the scale or changing the coordinate system. The result of such methods is slightly different since the transformation is applied at different points.

For our examples, we will use the `cont` dataset that we generated in the previous chapter with the following command, which contains three series of data values. The following command shows this:

```
cont <- data.frame(y=c(1:20,(1:20)^1.5,(1:20)^2), x=1:20,
group=rep(c(1,2,3),each=20))
```

We will first create a scatterplot with these values (*Figure 5.4(A)*), and then we will transform our *y* axis into `log10` values, as shown in the following command:

```
myScatter <- ggplot(data=cont, aes(x=x, y=y,
col=factor(group))) + geom_point()

myScatter + scale_y_log10()
```

In the preceding command, we used the scale function to transform the axis; this function directly corresponds to the `scale_y_continuous()` function but with log transformation of the data. Other similar functions that are also available are `scale_x_reverse()`, which inverts the values on the axis, and `scale_x_sqrt()`, which calculates the square root. You can see the resulting picture from our transformations in *Figure 5.4(B)*. Since, in this case, we have used the scale function, we have applied the transformation when creating the scale, so before that, properties such as breaks and ranges of data were created, and this means that the scale representing log-transformed data is done based on the newly transformed data. As mentioned earlier, we can also use coordinate transformation, but in this case, the transformation is applied, after which the scale is defined, which means that the scale that contained the original values is now represented on a log axis.

You can use coordinate transformation as shown in the following command and see the resulting plot in *Figure 5.4(C)*.

```
myScatter + coord_trans(y="log10")
```

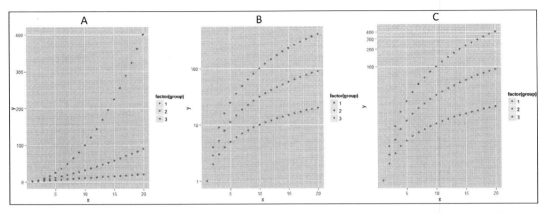

Figure 5.4: Example of scatterplots with default linear scales (A), a log-transformed y axis by changing the scale (B), and a log-transformed y axis by changing the coordinate system (C)

As illustrated, independent of the transformation method used, the data is represented in the same way in *Figure 5.4(B)* and *Figure 5.4(C)*, but the *y* axis scale is different; when transforming the scale, the axis contains log-transformed values, while, when changing coordinates, the values represented are the same as with the linear scale but represented in a log-transformed coordinate system.

Removing axis tick marks

In some cases, you may want to remove the axis tick marks since they may be redundant in your plot. For instance, if we look again at our dataset `dist`, and we plot only one distribution, we would end up with two labels: one for the data and one for the axis. In these cases, it may be handy to just delete the axis tick marks and use the axis label to define the type of data, as shown in the following command:

```
myBoxplot2 <- ggplot(subset(dist,group=="1"),
aes(x=group, y=value, fill=group)) + geom_boxplot()
myBoxplot2 + scale_x_discrete(breaks=NULL) +
xlab("Distribution of variable 1")
```

Legends

As we mentioned in *Chapter 3*, *The Layers and Grammar of Graphics*, legends are guides that represent the inverse of the applied scales and are used to trace back the plot elements to the aesthetic mapping. For this reason, legends are defined in ggplot2 as guides since they represent guides to the aesthetic mapping. The legend that is created by ggplot2 depends on the aesthetic mapping and the geometry that is used in the plot. For instance, *Figure 5.1* contains a continuous color scale, *Figure 5.2* contains boxplots, and *Figure 5.4* contains points.

Since legends are recreated by scale functions, most of the time you will need to use scale functions to modify the legend's appearance. In this section, we will go through how to change the four main aspects of legends: the title, labels, legend box, and legend position. But, first of all, let's see how we can remove the legend.

To remove the legend, you can use the guide argument of the scale function or directly use the guides() function dedicated to the manipulation of the guides. We will illustrate this using our boxplot example with the dist dataset:

```
### We create again our plot myBoxplot

myBoxplot <- ggplot(dist, aes(x=group, y=value, fill=group)) +
geom_boxplot()


### Remove legend with guides function

myBoxplot + guides(fill=FALSE)


### Remove legend with scale function

myBoxplot + scale_fill_discrete(guide=FALSE)
```

As illustrated in the preceding example, the command is quite straightforward, and you can use the guides or the scale function to leave out of the legend by setting the aesthetic to false. For instance, in this example, we have used the fill aesthetic mapped to the group variable, so we will need to use the scale function for the fill mapping of the scale_fill_discrete() discrete variable, or the guides() function with the fill mapping set to FALSE. The result from both commands will be the same, namely a boxplot without a legend.

For all the legend adjustments we will go through in this section, it is possible to use both the guides() and scale functions, but we will only work with the scale functions in our examples since this has the greater functionality of the two and guides() is comparatively straightforward.

The legend title

We have seen that the `name` argument of the scale function can be used for the axis label as well as the legend name. This may sound tricky but is actually quite simple. You will need to use the scale function for the aesthetic you want to manipulate. This aesthetic could be the axis, in which case the name argument will modify the axis label. Alternatively, the aesthetic could be the legend, in which case the name argument would modify the legend title. The following command shows a simple example of how to modify the axis name and the legend title, which will make this use clearer and generate the resulting plot of *Figure 5.5*:

```
myBoxplot +
scale_x_discrete(name="This is my x-axis") +
scale_fill_discrete(name="This is my legend")
```

This example modifies discrete variables in both cases; however, in the first case, we refer to the *x* aesthetic of the axis, while in the second case, the `fill` aesthetic is used to fill the boxplots with colors mapped to the `group` variable:

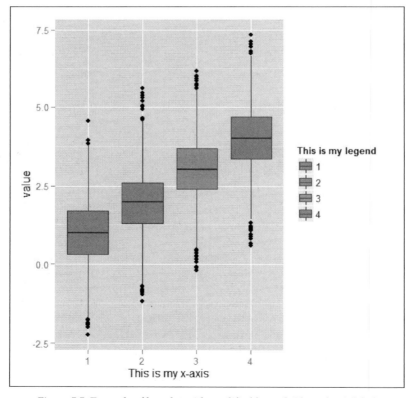

Figure 5.5: Example of boxplot with modified legend title and axis label

Not only can you use this method to change the legend title, you can actually remove it completely by simply providing an empty title name, as follows:

```
myBoxplot + scale_fill_discrete(name="")
```

As an alternative, you can also use the `theme()` function, as shown in the next command. However, in this case, you will remove all legend titles from all legends in your plot. We will look into the details of this function later on in this chapter. The following command shows this:

```
myBoxplot + theme(legend.title=element_blank())
```

Legend keys and key labels

The legend is composed of *keys*, the symbols relating the legend to the plot, and *key labels,* which describe what the keys represent. Generally, there are two main modifications to the default legend involving keys and key labels: first, to change the order of the elements, and next, to modify the text of the key labels. You can do these two modifications using the `breaks` and `labels` arguments of the scale function. The `breaks` argument defines which values appear in the legend, while the `labels` argument specifies the text that appears in the key labels. So, if you want to change the order of the keys in the legend, you can provide the order you want as a vector to the `breaks` argument. Just remember that the vector elements should match the dataset elements used to create the legend. The following command shows this:

```
myBoxplot + scale_fill_discrete(breaks=c("1","3","2","4"))
```

You can also directly inverse the order of the elements in the legend using the `guide_legend()` function. We have seen that the scale functions have an argument guide that can be used to control the legend's appearance and has the default value of `guide="legend"`. If you would like to modify the legend's appearance, there are also other guide options that can be used, but you will need to pass the explicit function name to guide, so the default value would correspond to `guide=guide_legend()`, and in the function body, you can change the default assignments. This function allows you to have profound control over the legend's appearance. A full listing of all available arguments can be found on the help page of the `?guide_legend` function. The `guide_legend()` function also provides the argument's reverse, which specifies that the legend order should be reversed. So, in our boxplot example, we could reverse the legend order with the following command:

```
myBoxplot + scale_fill_discrete(guide =
guide_legend(reverse=TRUE))
```

The same approach can also be used with the `guides()` function, as shown here:

```
myBoxplot + guides(fill = guide_legend(reverse=TRUE))
```

In order to change the key labels, we can use the `labels` argument to provide a vector of names matching `breaks`. Here, you can see the resulting boxplot example with a modified order of the legend elements and updated labels:

```
myBoxplot + scale_fill_discrete(breaks=c("1","3","2","4"),
labels=c("Dist 1","Dist 3","Dist 2","Dist 4"))
```

The resulting plot can be found in *Figure 5.6*:

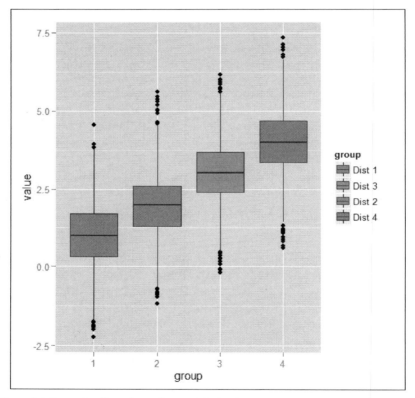

Figure 5.6: Example of boxplot with a modified order of the legend key and legend labels

Themes

In ggplot2, you have access to a series of functions that enable detailed control of plot appearance. These functions are called themes in ggplot2 and can be used to control nondata components of plots, such as the axis font, plot background, and position of the legend. This means that they do not affect how the data is represented in terms of geometry or how it is transformed by the scales. The main function in this respect is the theme() function. This function is very complex since it allows you to specify all the different details contributing to the plot appearance as well as generating your own format and style. In the next few pages, we will see some illustrative examples that demonstrate what you can produce, but for more details, you should definitely have a look at the document page at http://docs.ggplot2.org/current/theme.html.

In ggplot2, you have two built-in themes available that can be applied directly to your plot: theme_grey(), which is the default theme, has a gray background with white gridlines, while theme_bw() has a white background and black gridlines. You can use these predefined themes as normal plot elements that are added on top of the plot. Here, you can see an example of how to use them, and in *Figure 5.7*, you can see the resulting plots.

```
myBoxplot + theme_grey()
myBoxplot + theme_bw()
```

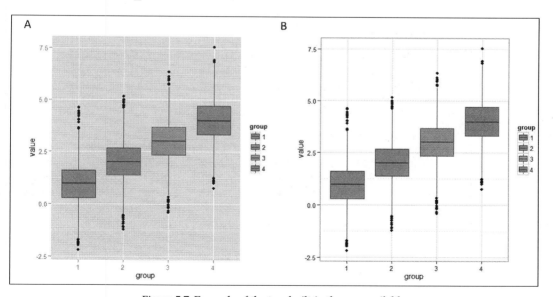

Figure 5.7: Example of the two built-in themes available

If, on the other hand, you want to have different specifications for the themes available, then you will need to use the `theme()` function and specify the elements that you want to modify. In the `theme()` function, you will need to specify two things: the element of the plot that you want to modify (for instance, the axis character, background, and so on) and the theme element, which is basically a function that allows you to provide formatting specifications of that particular theme element. You can select three different theme elements depending on what you want to change in the plot. You will be introduced to the different themes available in the upcoming sections.

In our examples, we will take a look at how to use the `theme()` function to personalize the legend, axis, and plot background. After some examples, you will have a clearer idea of how to use these functions and what kinds of personalization you have available to you when specifying the plot layout.

Themes for the legend

You can use the theme function to modify legends and specify the legend background, its position, and its margins. For instance, you can add a rectangular box around the legend of our boxplot with the following command; the resulting plot is represented in *Figure 5.8(A)*.

```
myBoxplot + theme(legend.background = element_rect(color =
"black"))
```

In the preceding command, we used the `legend.background()` theme element to specify the legend box and its color. To do this, we have used the rectangular theme element `element_rect()`. This element is often used for backgrounds and borders. Other theme elements available include `element_line()` for line elements, `element_text()` for text elements, and `element_blank()` that does not draw anything and can be used to remove elements.

> You are probably wondering why by selecting `color="black"`, we do not end up with a black background. The logic behind this code is the same as for some of the `geom` as the bar plots and boxplots for instance. You can use the `color` argument to define the border, while you would use the `fill` argument to define the filling color of the box. So, for instance, if we want to change the legend background, you can use the following command:
>
> ```
> myBoxplot + theme(legend.background =
> element_rect(fill="gray90"))
> ```

As well as the legend background, you can also control the key background, that is, the background of the legend keys, which, by default, in `ggplot2`, is gray. In order to do that, we would need to use the `legend.key` argument, as shown here:

```
myBoxplot + theme(legend.key = element_rect(color = "black"))
myBoxplot + theme(legend.key = element_rect(fill = "yellow"))
```

In the first example, we included a black box around each legend key, as shown in *Figure 5.8(B)*, while in the second example, we changed the key background, as shown in *Figure 5.8(C)*.

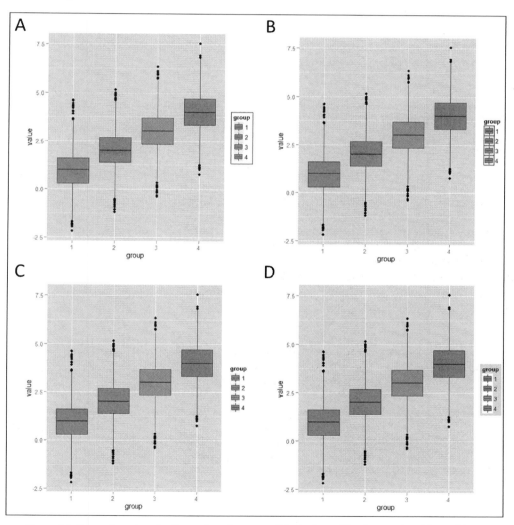

Figure 5.8: Examples using the theme function to modify the legend background and legend keys

You can also combine the element we just introduced to make a nice theme for the legend, where the default key background (gray) is replaced with a white background and the legend box is filled with the same background gray of the plot area. You can see the resulting plot in *Figure 5.8(D)*. The following command shows this:

```
myBoxplot + theme(legend.background =
element_rect(fill="gray90"), legend.key = element_rect(fill =
"white"))
```

You can also control the space around the legend using the `legend.margin()` argument. For instance, you can increase the area around the legend to 3 cm with the following command:

```
require(grid)
myBoxplot + theme(legend.margin = unit(3, "cm"))
```

Just notice that the `legend.margin` argument needs an object of the `unit` class that can be created with the `unit()` function, so you need to load the package grid that contains this function. You can see the resulting plot in *Figure 5.9*, where you can see how this space is rendered in the plot:

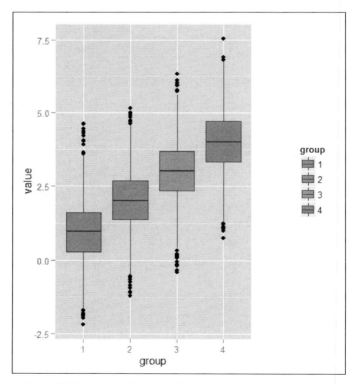

Figure 5.9: Example of legend with increased margin space of 3cm

It is also possible to control the legend text by choosing, for instance, its size, its position, its color, and its font. Here, you can see an example of applying such changes to our plot:

```
myBoxplot + theme(legend.text = element_text(size = 20, color =
"red", angle = 45, face = "italic"))
```

As illustrated, in this case we had to use the `legend.text` argument, but in order to modify it, we used the `element_text()` theme function since, in this case, we are modifying a text element. We were also able to specify the angle at which we can rotate the text; we will see that this option can be quite useful in the next subsection to rotate axis labels. We also used the `face` argument to specify the font of the text. The same argument can also be used to change a font in another piece of text within the plots, such as the legend title or the axis text. You can see the resulting plot in *Figure 5.10*.

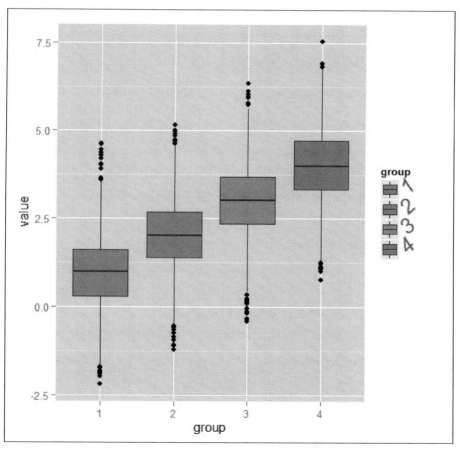

Figure 5.10: Example of legend with modified text in the key labels

Finally, you can, of course, also modify the legend position. In this respect, ggplot2 is really flexible since it allows you to not only choose from different standard positions, but also place the legend within the plot area very easily. In order to do that, we can use the legend.position argument and specify the position desired. You can choose between the traditional positions available in other graphic packages, namely left, right, top, bottom, and none if you do not have a legend. Alternatively, you can specify a vector defining the relative position within the plot area containing values from 0 to 1, with c(0,0) being the bottom-left position and c(1,1) being the top-right position. The following are two simple examples of its application: the first one with the legend at the bottom and the second one with the legend in the centre of the plot area.

```
myBoxplot + theme(legend.position = "bottom")
myBoxplot + theme(legend.position = c(0.5, 0.5))
```

You can see the resulting plot in *Figure 5.11*:

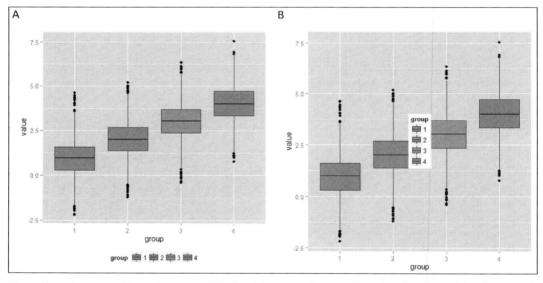

Figure 5.11: Examples of legends with modified positions at the bottom (A) and in the centre of the plot area (B)

Themes for the axis and title

The theme function available in `ggplot2` also allows you to specify the details of how the axis text elements are represented, for instance, by controlling the type of characters, their size, and position. Here, you can see an example of formatting the axis tick marks, where we change the `color` of the text to `blue` and the character to `italic`.

```
myBoxplot + theme(axis.text = element_text(color = "blue", face =
"italic"))
```

As illustrated, in this case, we used `element_text()` since we modified text elements and used the `axis.text` argument to allow us to modify elements along all axes at the same time. You can see the results in *Figure 5.12(A)*. Generally speaking, within the different arguments that you will have available for the `theme()` function, you will find arguments that control elements of a certain class. In this case, `axis.text` affects all axis elements, and further, you will find arguments that can be used to control specific elements within a class as, for instance, `axis.text.y`, which can be used to modify only the *y* axis. You can see an example of such a modification in the following command, where we will modify the angle of the text to make the caption of the *y* axis horizontal and increase `size` as well:

```
myBoxplot + theme(axis.title.y = element_text(size = rel(1.5),
angle = 0))
```

The result is shown in *Figure 5.12(B)*:

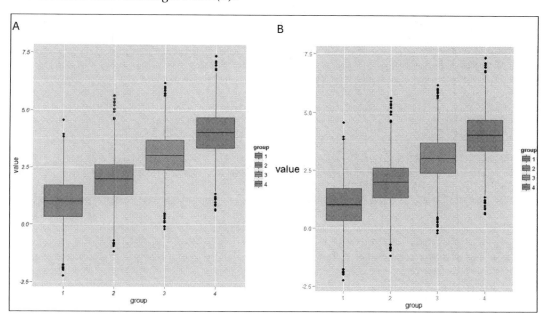

Figure 5.12: Examples of axis layout modifications—axis tick marks (A) and axis label (B)

The same idea also applies to titles. In fact, you can use the argument title, which allows you to control all the `title` elements in the plot. This means that you can, for instance, change the axis title, the legend title, and the plot's main title using only one command. This can be quite handy since, in many situations, you will want to have a homogenous layout with all titles formatted in the same way, without using several different functions for the individual elements. So, in the example, we will change `size` and `color` of the title elements. The following command shows this

```
myBoxplot + labs(title="This is my boxplot") +
theme(title = element_text(size = rel(1.5), color="blue"))
```

On the other hand, if you need to modify only one of the title elements, you have the option to use more specific arguments, for instance, in the following example, we will modify only the main title text.

```
myBoxplot + labs(title="This is my boxplot") +
theme(plot.title = element_text(size = rel(1.5), color="blue"))
```

The resulting plot of the command prior to the preceding command is found in *Figure 5.13(A)*. You also have the resulting plot of the preceding command in *Figure 5.13(B)*, and as illustrated, the axis titles remain unchanged.

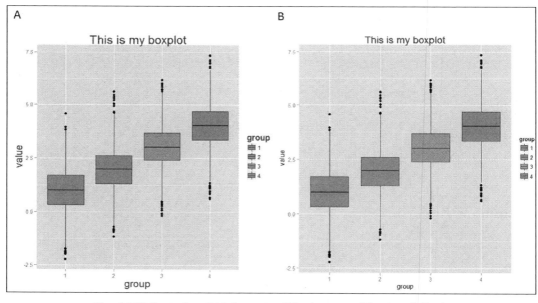

Figure 5.13: Examples of title layout modifications—modification of all title elements (A) and only of the main title (B)

At the beginning of this section, we mentioned the `element_blank()` function as a way to generate an element that does not draw anything. Keep in mind that you can always use this element to delete components of the plot that you don´t need and that this applies to titles, axis elements, and so on. For instance in our boxplot, we have the grouping information already contained in the legend, so we could think about removing the groups for the *x* axis so that we can use the blank element to delete them as shown here:

```
myBoxplot + theme(axis.text.x = element_blank())
```

As illustrated in the following plot, this produces a plot without the axis text, but the tick marks and the axis title are still there. However, since we have removed the text, we don't actually need these marks, so we can remove both the tick marks as well as the title as shown here:

```
myBoxplot + theme(axis.text.x = element_blank(), axis.ticks.x = element_blank(),axis.title.x = element_blank())
```

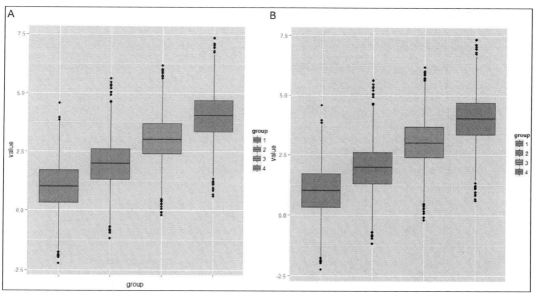

Figure 5.14: Examples of removing axis elements—only the x axis text (A) and x axis text, tick marks, and title components (B)

The results of both code statements are shown in *Figure 5.14*. Now you know how you can combine several theme elements on the same call and have also gained an understanding of how you can use the `theme()` function not only to modify, but also to remove plot components that you don´t need.

We have seen so far how you can modify the text and title of the axis, but as you know, axes are not only composed of these components. We can, in fact, also modify the layout of the axes themselves: the appearance of the line along the plot axis as well as the axis tick marks, which, so far, we have only deleted in the previous example. For instance, we can modify the axis line as shown here to change its `color` and make it much thicker:

```
myBoxplot + theme(axis.line = element_line(size = 3, color =
"red", linetype = "solid"))
```

In this case, we had to use `element_line()` since the axis element we want to modify is a line. You can see the outcome in *Figure 5.15(A)*. We can also apply a modification to the tick marks, as already mentioned. There are several arguments that can control the axis tick marks, but for the most part, the most useful modifications to tick marks are probably `margin` and `length`. The `length` element simply controls the length of tick marks for both axes, and you can provide the length as a unit object from the grid package. The `margin`, which you can also provide as a unit object, defines the distance between the tick marks and the text of the axis. You can see here an example of these two modifications:

```
require(grid)
myBoxplot + theme(axis.ticks.length = unit(.85,
"cm"),axis.ticks.margin=unit(.85, "cm"))
```

The resulting plot is shown in *Figure 5.15(B)*:

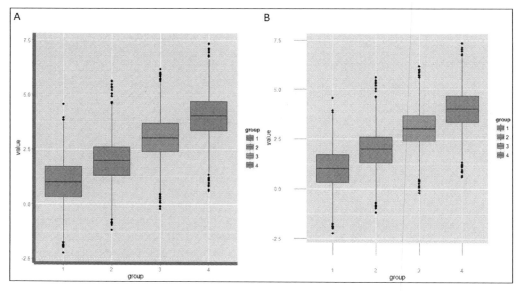

Figure 5.15: Example modification of axis line (A) and axis tick marks (B)

Themes for the plot background

The theme() function allows you to control the background appearance of the plot. Here, there are a number of aspects that can be useful to modify, but the most important, by far, are background and the panel grid. The panel grid refers to guidelines drawn by default in ggplot2. Using the theme() function, you can, for instance, control the guideline appearance and the color.

 One thing you should keep in mind is that in ggplot2 panels, there are two different grids, a major grid, which delimits the major unit steps, such as the ones represented on the axis by the tick marks, and a minor grid, which traces lines along the intermediate unit steps.

Here, you can see two different examples of how to modify these parameters. There is some variability as the grid behavior and appearance depend on the kind of data being represented; for factor data, just as we have on the x axis of our box plot, we only have major grid lines since we do not have intermediate units between the groups. As a comparison, had we applied the same formatting to a more traditional scatterplot, where there is continuous data on both axes, there would be both major and minor gridlines. As an example, we will use the myScatter plot, which we created earlier in this chapter.

```
# Example with a boxplot

myBoxplot + theme(panel.background = element_rect(fill =
"gray80"), panel.grid.major = element_line(color = "blue"),
panel.grid.minor = element_line(color = "white", linetype =
"dotted", size=1))


# Example with a scatter plot

myScatter + theme(panel.background = element_rect(fill =
"gray80"), panel.grid.major = element_line(color = "blue"),
panel.grid.minor = element_line(color = "white", linetype =
"dotted", size=1))
```

You can see the resulting plots in *Figure 5.16*. Changing the appearance of the grids presented in the plot panel may be quite useful when you change the default color of the background since you may end up in the situation where the appearance of the grid does not have significant enough contrast.

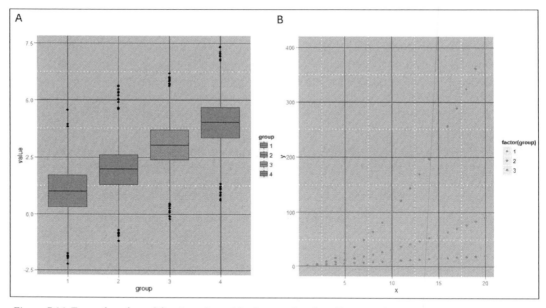

Figure 5.16: Examples of modification of panel background and gridlines in a boxplot (A) and a scatterplot (B)

As already discussed, you can also use `element_blank()` to eliminate the grid if you don't want to have it in the panel. Here, you can find a simple example of how to use this option:

```
myScatter + theme(panel.background = element_rect(fill =
"gray80"), panel.grid.major = element_blank(), panel.grid.minor =
element_blank())
```

Additionally, for the panel background, you also have the option to specify the actual plot background and border. In this case, we would be modifying the area around the plot window using the `plot.background` argument. In our example, we will modify both the `color` of this area as well as its border, which corresponds to the border of the plot figure:

```
myScatter + theme(plot.background = element_rect(fill = "green",
color="red", size=2, linetype = "dotted"))
```

You can see the resulting plot represented in *Figure 5.17*.

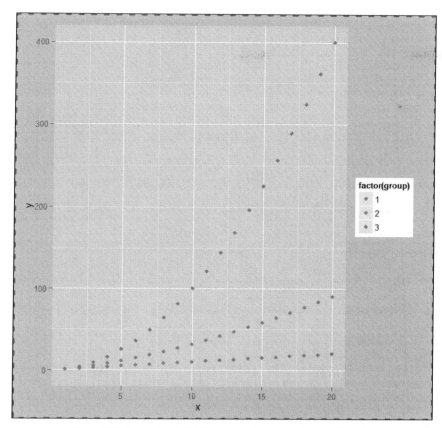

Figure 5.17: Example of plot background and border modification

Themes with facets

When using facets, you can apply the same formatting style that we have already discussed, so, for instance, the following command will create a plot where each facet will have a blue background:

```
myScatter + facet_grid(. ~ group) + theme(panel.background =
element_rect(fill = "lightblue"))
```

On the other hand, you also have additional formatting options available where you make a facet plot. If you are already familiar with the `lattice` package, you may know that on the top of facets is a title strip area. In the strip area, you can, for instance, control the text as well as the background, as shown here:

```
myScatter + facet_grid(. ~ group) + theme(strip.background =
element_rect(color = "lightblue", fill = "pink",size = 3,
linetype = "dashed"))
```

In this simple example, we have changed the background color of the facet title strip area and its border. You can see the resulting picture in *Figure 5.18*:

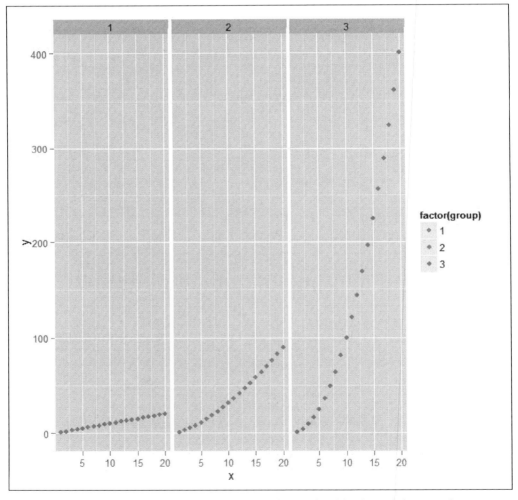

Figure 5.18: Example of modification of color background and border with facet panel strip

If you have a longer title in the strip area, it may turn out to be useful to change the text size and its orientation. For instance, you can use the `labeller` argument of the facet function to specify a variable name for the labels of the facets, which can be useful in some cases but may increase the text length. For instance, we can then change `size` and the orientation of such text as shown here:

```
myScatter + facet_grid(. ~ group, labeller = label_both) +
theme(strip.text.x = element_text(color = "red", angle = 45, size
= 15, hjust = 0.5, vjust = 0.5))
```

You can see the resulting plot in *Figure 5.19*:

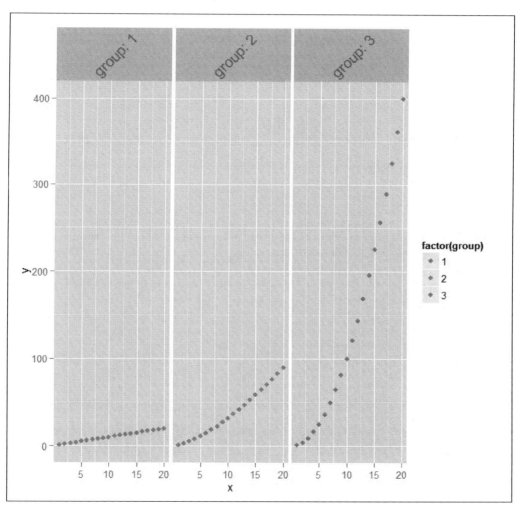

Figure 5.19: Example of text modification in the panel strip

Finally, here's another layout property specific to facets is the margin between the panels. In this case as well, you can modify such a space, for instance, to increase or decrease the space between the facets, as shown here:

```
myScatter + facet_grid(. ~ group) + theme(panel.margin = unit(2,
"cm"))
```

You can see the result in *Figure 5.20*.

As we did in other examples, space units can be provided to use the unit() function from the grid package. It can also be used to specify the space in different units; more details can be found on the function's help page.

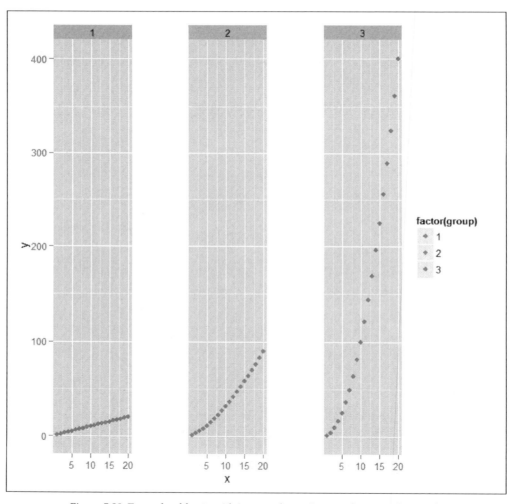

Figure 5.20: Example of facets with increased margin space between the panels

In addition to increasing the space, you can also set the margin space to 0, and in this case, you will have the facets completely connected with each other, providing an interesting effect of a singular plot but with three different *x* axes that start over after each other. The following command shows this:

```
myScatter + facet_grid(. ~ group) + theme(panel.margin = unit(0,
"cm"))
```

You can see this alternative plot in *Figure 5.21*:

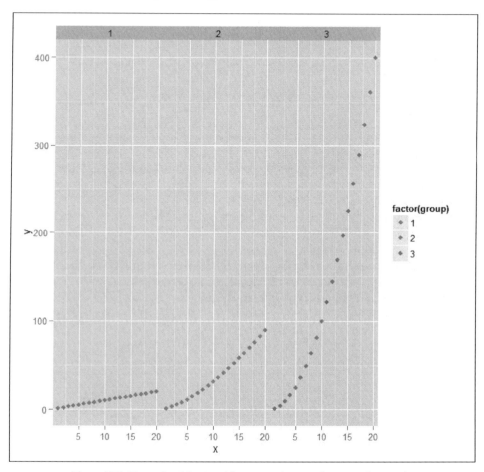

Figure 5.21: Example of facets without margin space between the panels

Further reading

Additional examples can be found on the respective help pages of ggplot2. Here, you can find examples of the most important options and scales:

- Axis labels and legend titles: http://docs.ggplot2.org/0.9.2.1/labs.html
- Scales for *x* and *y* axes for discrete values: http://docs.ggplot2.org/current/scale_discrete.html
- Scales for *x* and *y* axes for continuous values: http://docs.ggplot2.org/current/scale_continuous.html
- Theme elements: http://docs.ggplot2.org/current/theme.html

Summary

In this chapter, we went through the most important layout changes that you can apply to your plot. We saw how you can personalize the plot title and the axis labels, use the scale functions to modify the axis plot scales, and make axis transformations. We then saw what kind of modifications you can apply to the legends and, finally, we saw the different options available within theme selections. What you should have at the end of this chapter is a good understanding of what kind of changes you can make to the default layout of the plot as well as how to perform them. You can use this chapter as a small library of examples to go through if you want to change something but can't remember how to do it. In the next chapter, we will have a look at how we can save plots in different formats on your hard drive as well as how different plots can be arranged in R in a single picture.

6
Plot Output

In this chapter, we will take a look at the different methods you can use to save or manipulate the output generated with ggplot2. We will cover the different methods of displaying multiple plots in a unique plot page and how to save the plots that you have created on your hard drive.

Multiple plots in one page

If you are already familiar with the graphics package, you know that in R, you have the opportunity to create plot windows on which you can arrange multiple plots. In ggplot2, there is no single function available to do that, but you will need to become familiar with certain basic concepts of the grid package, which was used to build ggplot2. In grid, you have the possibility of defining viewports, which are rectangular regions on a graphics device, and plots can be assigned to these regions. In order to do that, we can use a grid function called viewport(). Using this method, you have two main ways of combining multiple plots:

- Arranging plots by specifying the plot position in terms of rows and columns
- Specifying the exact position of each plot

In the following sections, we will see examples of both methods.

Arranging plots in rows and columns

This approach of combining plots is very likely to be more convenient, and it will probably fit most of your needs. If you are already familiar with graphics, this method is very similar to the use of the par() function. In this approach, we simply define a plot area as columns and rows by specifying how many rows and columns we need, and then assign each plot to a specific area. As an example, we will recreate *Figure 3.2*, which was used in *Chapter 3*, *The Layers and Grammar of Graphics*, to illustrate the concepts of layers in ggplot2. Since you are already familiar with the different functions that enable you to modify the plot details, we will not discuss this point any longer, but we will focus on how to arrange the plots created in a single plot window. Nevertheless, you can take a look at the code used to realize single plots and use them as additional examples of personalization of the plot's appearance. This example was realized using data from the Orange dataset available in R. As a starting point, we will create the four individual plots, as shown here, but remember that you will also need to load grid for the following steps:

```
library(ggplot2)
library(grid)


data(Orange)


x1<- ggplot(Orange, aes(age, circumference)) +
geom_point(aes(colour=factor(Tree)))


### Remove the legend
x2 <- x1 + theme(legend.position = "none")


### Remove aesthetic
x3 <- ggplot(Orange, aes(age, circumference)) + geom_point()


### Plot without data
x4 <- x3 + theme(panel.border = element_rect(linetype = "solid",
colour = "black"))


x5 <- x3 + theme(axis.ticks = element_blank(), axis.text.x =
element_blank(), axis.text.y = element_blank(), panel.grid.major =
element_blank(), panel.grid.minor = element_blank(),
panel.background = element_blank()) + ylab("") + xlab("")
```

As illustrated, we first created a basic, complete plot, x1, and then we modified the plot by changing its appearance. When working with plots, it is often convenient to save their ggplot2 objects as variables and reference them as needed. This coding style makes it easier to rearrange plots into different positions and makes your code easier to read. To combine these plots in one window, we will first specify to the grid function that we want to define four different plot areas, which can be considered as a grid of two rows and two columns. Then, we will assign the desired plot to each section, as shown here:

```
pushViewport(viewport(layout = grid.layout(nrow=2, ncol=2)))
print(x5, vp = viewport(layout.pos.row = 1, layout.pos.col = 1))
print(x4, vp = viewport(layout.pos.row = 1, layout.pos.col = 2))
print(x3, vp = viewport(layout.pos.row = 2, layout.pos.col = 1))
print(x2, vp = viewport(layout.pos.row = 2, layout.pos.col = 2))
```

A tree of pushed viewports can be maintained by the grid in each device, allowing navigation between plots. A viewport object must be pushed onto the viewport tree before it has any effect on drawing. The pushViewport() function allows you to add viewport objects to the viewport tree and, in this function, we specify that we want to create a viewport with a layout composed of two rows and two columns. Afterwards, we assign plots to each plot area of the viewport by specifying its location in the plot area. As mentioned, the resulting picture is *Figure 3.2* from *Chapter 3, The Layers and Grammar of Graphics*.

In the layout.pos.row and layout.pos.col arguments, you can specify a single position in the plot grid, as we did in our example, or a vector of length 2 units, which defines a range of rows or columns on which the plot should be represented. If one of these arguments is missing, it will be assumed that the plot will be present in all available rows and columns. For instance, we can modify *Figure 3.2* by stretching the x4 plot across all the columns and removing the x5 plot. We can do that by simply removing the column argument, as shown here:

```
pushViewport(viewport(layout = grid.layout(2, 2)))
print(x4, vp = viewport(layout.pos.row = 1))
print(x3, vp = viewport(layout.pos.row = 2, layout.pos.col = 1))
print(x2, vp = viewport(layout.pos.row = 2, layout.pos.col = 2))
```

This code will produce the plot represented in *Figure 6.1*. As previously mentioned, you can also specify a range of columns, so, for instance, in this case, we could also have specified that the x4 plot should be represented in the first row from the first to the second columns, as shown here:

```
pushViewport(viewport(layout = grid.layout(2, 2)))
print(x4, vp = viewport(layout.pos.row = 1,layout.pos.col =
c(1,2)))
print(x3, vp = viewport(layout.pos.row = 2, layout.pos.col = 1))
print(x2, vp = viewport(layout.pos.row = 2, layout.pos.col = 2))
```

This code will also generate the plot in *Figure 6.1*:

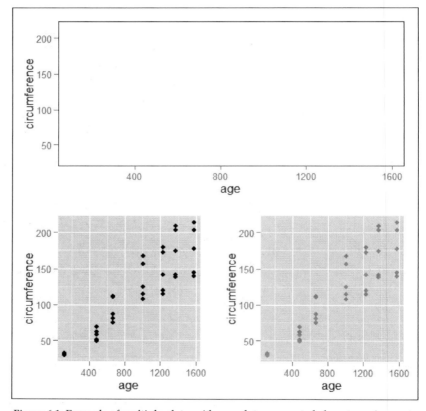

Figure 6.1: Example of multiple plots, with one plot represented along two viewports

Specifying the plot position

In the previous section, we considered the case where you have several plots that you want to visualize in a single window, but you want to leave the plots substantially separated and next to each other. In some cases, you may need to control the position of the plots more precisely, for instance, if you want to partly superimpose the plots. This can also be realized with the `viewport()` function, but instead of specifying the position of the plot as rows and columns, we can also provide the exact position to the functions. In this function, you have the x, y, width, and `height` arguments available, which allow you to specify the x and y locations and `width` and `height` of the plot, respectively. The default unit of these parameters is **Normalized Parent Coordinates (NPC)**, where the coordinates (0, 0) represent the origins of the viewport's width and height of one unit. For instance, the position (0.5, 0.5) represents the center of the viewport. You can also specify the plot position in other units using the `unit()` function from the `grid` packages when providing the arguments. We already encountered this in the previous chapter. For additional details, you can take a look at the function help page by typing ?unit. Alternatively, the `viewport()` function also provides the `default.units` argument, where you can specify the unit you are using, and this unit will be used if the x, y, width, and `height` arguments are specified as numeric values instead of the `unit()` function. In order to know which units you can use, you can refer to the list of units available in the `unit()` function help page.

To demonstrate this approach, we will consider a simple example with the `count` dataset, which we already used in the previous chapters. Let's assume that we have our data represented in the normal scale and the log scale as well. In some cases, you will probably need to look at both plots at the same time since you may be interested in the behavior of the data when represented in the log scale. In our example here, we will create the data, represent it in the linear scale and the log scale for the y axis, and then include the plot in the log scale in a corner of the linear scale plot so that the plots of the data are visible next to each other. The following code shows this:

```
### We create the dataset
cont <- data.frame(y=c(1:20,(1:20)^1.5,(1:20)^2),
    x=1:20,
    group=rep(c(1,2,3),each=20))


### We plot the data in two scatterplots, in linear and log-scale
```

```
myScatter <- ggplot(data=cont, aes(x=x, y=y,
col=factor(group))) + geom_point()


myScatterLog <- myScatter + scale_y_log10() +
theme(legend.position="none")


### We combine the two plots
print(myScatter, vp = viewport(width = 1, height = 1, x=0.5, y =
0.5))
print(myScatterLog, vp = viewport(width = 0.4, height = 0.4,
x=0.315, y = 0.76))
```

In the resulting plot in *Figure 6.2*, you will notice how we removed the legend from
the plot in the log scale since, with this representation, it is clear that the two plots
refer to the same data and the legend applies to both of them. As illustrated, when
representing the data with this approach, we obtain a different visual effect as
compared to having the plots simply next to each other. This simple example shows
how to control the exact position of your plot, but, of course, the possibilities are
unlimited. You can start from here and try different possibilities of finding the best
way to represent your data.

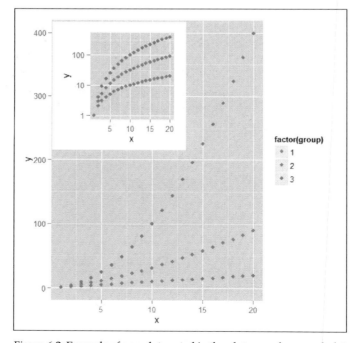

Figure 6.2: Example of one plot nested in the plot area of a second plot

Saving plots to a file

In this section, we will take a look at the different methods available of saving your plots. Most of these concepts apply to all plots realized in R although we will also consider the `ggsave()` function that is specific to the `ggplot2()` package. In R, there are three ways that you can use to save created plots:

- Saving the plot manually by way of the device window system (could be different between operating systems)
- Saving the plot to a file without rendering the plot
- Saving the plot after rendering the plot

We will take a look at the different methods in the upcoming sections. Just keep in mind that when you save a file as a plot, the file with the specified filename will be saved in your working directory. Be careful since, if you already have a file with the same name, it will be overwritten without any warnings from R, so if you run the code in these examples, just verify that your working directory does not contain files with the same name as the plot that we will save.

Saving the plot manually

An easy way to save your plot to a file is to do it manually in the R GUI. After running the code that generates the plot, R will render the plot in a device window, which will open in the R console. At this point, by selecting the graph window, you will have access to the dedicated menu, where, in the *File* section, you can find the saving options. You can choose between different file formats, such as PNG, JPEG, and PDF, as well as save the plot in the clipboard or print the plot directly. Alternatively, you can also right-click on the plot itself, and you will be able to also copy the plot to the clipboard or save it as a metafile or bitmap.

Saving the plot to a file without rendering it

In some cases, you may want to save the file directly from code without manually saving it. This approach can, for instance, be very useful if you have scripts running and producing standard plots. In this case, you can embed code in your scripts to do analysis and produce standard plots. There are several different functions that can save your plot in a variety of formats. What these functions do is open a graphical device and render your plot in the device until the device is closed. For this reason, the plot will not be rendered on the R console but will be saved directly in the graphical device. There are several functions that allow you to create different file formats, the most important of them being PNG, PDF, and JPEG, which are listed here with some of their main arguments:

- `png(filename, width, height)`
- `pdf(file, width, height)`
- `jpeg(filename, width, height)`

You can find a complete list of the devices available by running `?Devices`.

All these functions work in a very similar way so, in our examples, we will take a look at the `pdf()` function.

Saving a single plot

If you want to save, for instance, a plot in a PDF file, you can use the following command:

```
pdf("myFile.pdf")
ggplot(data=cont, aes(x=x, y=y, col=factor(group))) + geom_point()
dev.off()
```

This code will create a file called `myFile.pdf` in the current working directory, in which the plot will be saved. Keep in mind that even if you are using the `pdf()` function, you will need to specify the file extension in the function; otherwise, the file created will not be saved as PDF. After running the `pdf()` function, simply run the plot code you want to include in `myFile.pdf`, and it will be saved to the file. After you have run all the plots you need, you can close the device with `dev.off()`. The first part of the code, where we used the `pdf()` function, is the part that should be changed if you want to create a different file, while the remaining part of the code is independent of the type of device selected. So, for instance, if you wanted to create a PNG file, you can do so in the following way:

```
png("myFile.png")
```

```
ggplot(data=cont, aes(x=x, y=y, col=factor(group)))+geom_point()
dev.off()
```

In the simple examples that we have considered, we have been working on the console when creating the file. Alternatively, you can also include such code in a script that is run automatically to create plots. So, if you are running the code as a script, you will need to explicitly print the plot, as shown here:

```
png("myFile2.png")
print(ggplot(data=cont, aes(x=x, y=y,
col=factor(group))) + geom_point())
dev.off()
```

Saving multiple plots on the same PDF file

One very interesting feature of PDF files is the possibility of saving multiple plots in them just by saving them in different pages. In order to do that, you need to simply add multiple plots one after the other, as shown here:

```
pdf("myFile2.pdf")
ggplot(data=cont, aes(x=x, y=y, col=factor(group))) + geom_point()
ggplot(Orange, aes(age, circumference)) +
geom_point(aes(colour=factor(Tree)))
dev.off()
```

This code will create a PDF file with two pages, each containing one of the plots. This method does not work when you manipulate the viewport manually, for instance, using the `viewport()` function, as shown in the previous section, since each new plot generated overwrites the previous one. So, for instance, if you want to create a PDF file containing *Figure 6.1* on the first page and *Figure 6.2* on the second page, the code to be run would be as follows:

```
pdf("myFile3.pdf")
pushViewport(viewport(layout = grid.layout(2, 2)))
print(x4, vp = viewport(layout.pos.row = 1,layout.pos.col =
c(1,2)))
print(x3, vp = viewport(layout.pos.row = 2, layout.pos.col = 1))
print(x2, vp = viewport(layout.pos.row = 2, layout.pos.col = 2))

print(myScatter, vp = viewport(width = 1, height = 1, x=0.5, y =
0.5))
print(myScatterLog, vp = viewport(width = 0.4, height = 0.4,
x=0.315, y = 0.76))
dev.off()
```

But, in this case, you will produce a PDF file containing only the last created plot. The reason for this is that `grid` will add the plots on top of each other. This happens in the R console when you create several plots one after the other, but only the last one is visible in the device. In order to solve the problem, you must simply specify to the `grid` function that the plot should be produced in a new page and not by overwriting the previous one with the `grid.newpage()` command. The following code will create the right PDF files with the two plots in separate pages:

```
pdf("myFile3.pdf")
pushViewport(viewport(layout = grid.layout(2, 2)))
print(x4, vp = viewport(layout.pos.row = 1,layout.pos.col = c(1,2)))
print(x3, vp = viewport(layout.pos.row = 2, layout.pos.col = 1))
print(x2, vp = viewport(layout.pos.row = 2, layout.pos.col = 2))


grid.newpage()


print(myScatter, vp = viewport(width = 1, height = 1, x=0.5, y =
0.5))
print(myScatterLog, vp = viewport(width = 0.4, height = 0.4, x=0.315,
y = 0.76))
dev.off()
```

Finally, in in the `pdf()` function of each device function, you can also specify a number of different arguments. Here, the most important ones are `width` and `height`, which define the `width` and `height` parameters of the graphics region in inches, with a default value of 7. You can use these two parameters to modify the appearance of the graph, for instance, to modify the ratio between the two axes. You can also find additional arguments for a more precise fine-tuning of the file properties in the help pages of the individual functions.

Saving the plot after rendering it

I find creating the files using the method illustrated in the previous section very convenient and, often, this is the easiest way to save plots, but some R users do not really find the approach practical as you need to refine the properties of your plot until the desired picture is obtained and then recreate it in order to save it in a file. In this respect, it may be of interest to some R users to save the plot directly from the rendered plot in the active window of the console. In this way, as soon as you are happy with your work, you can save it directly in a file without recreating the plot. Indeed, this may be useful if you are working with very complex plots that can require time to generate. In such cases, you need not wait again for the plot to be drawn. In order to do that, you can use the following two functions with some of their arguments:

- `dev.copy(device, file)`
- `ggsave(filename, width, height)`

These functions are substantially similar; however, an important difference is that when using the `dev.copy()` function, you should specify the type of device (and the type of file to create) in the function, and then you can specify all the arguments of that device function. On the other hand, in `ggsave()`, you can simply specify the file extension in the filename argument, and the function will automatically select the device function needed. Also, `ggsave()` provides you with additional arguments to specify the file's properties.

 Remember that these functions with their default arguments will only save the last plot that you displayed.

You can create the `myFile.pdf` file of the previous example, as shown here, using the following two functions:

```
#### Saving a rendered plot with dev.copy()
ggplot(data=cont, aes(x=x, y=y, col=factor(group))) + geom_point()
dev.copy(pdf, file="myFile.pdf")
dev.off()


#### Saving a rendered plot with ggsave()
ggplot(data=cont, aes(x=x, y=y, col=factor(group))) + geom_point()
ggsave(file="myFile.pdf")
```

As illustrated, when using the `dev.copy()` function after all plots are saved you need to close the device using the `dev.off()` function. There is no such need with `ggsave()`, where you only need to provide the filename.

Further reading

- *R Graphics (2nd edition), P. Murrell, CRC Press*
- Documentation of the grid package for functions: `?unit`, `?viewport`, and `?pushViewport`
- Documentation of the device functions of the `grDevices` package: `?Devices`
- Documentation of the `ggsave()` function: `?ggsave`
- Tips on how to save your plots: `http://blog.revolutionanalytics.com/2009/01/10-tips-for-making-your-r-graphics-look-their-best.html`

Summary

In this chapter, we saw how you can manipulate the organization of the plot in the plot area. This is useful when you want to place several plots next to each other or if you want to include a small plot inset within the plot area of another graph. We also saw how you can save your plot in a file, ranging from manually saving the plot up to including the saving options in a script file that can be executed. In the last chapter, we will see a few applications of `ggplot2` that also involve the use of other R packages. We will see how mapped data can be plotted in `ggplot2` objects and how matrix scatterplots and heat maps can be created.

7
Special Applications of ggplot2

In this chapter, we will see some examples of applications of `ggplot2` for creating particular kinds of plots. We will see how it is possible to include maps in plots as well as add data to such maps; we will see how to draw scatterplot matrices to represent the relationships between different variables; finally, we will see how to generate heat maps. Although, in principle, it is also possible to realize these plots using only `ggplot2`, in some cases it is a lot more convenient and faster to use additional packages where the particular plot layout is already implemented.

Plotting maps with ggplot2 and ggmap

In `ggplot2`, it is possible to include maps as well as map data within a plot. This can be done thanks to certain `ggplot2` functions that allow the combination of typical `ggplot2` elements with data from the `maps` package. Alternatively, `ggmap`, a dedicated R package, was developed by David Kahle and Hadley Wickham and enables the easy inclusion of map data in `ggplot2` graphs using map data provided on the Internet.

Mapping representations with ggplot2 and maps

The maps package is an R package that contains cartographic data for some individual countries as well as for the entire world, including example datasets that can be used to combine data to map representations. The limitation of this data is related to the limited maps available, consequently limiting the plots that can be realized with this approach. In addition to this, you should also keep in mind that these maps may be quite outdated. The maps currently available in the package are as follows:

- world: This is a map of the entire world
- usa: This is a map of the US coast
- state: This is a map of the USA at the state level
- county: This is a map of the USA at the county level
- italy: This is a map of Italy
- france: This is a map of France
- nz: This is a map of New Zealand

Additionally in the package, maps are also provided along with databases with information about, and positions of, cities, such as *us.cities* and *world.cities*. The representation of map data as well as the inclusion of additional data to a cartographic representation can be very complex, so we will just go through general examples. If you are interested in a more detailed description, you will find links in the *Further reading* section at the end of the chapter.

The general way of plotting maps with ggplot2 is creating a plot element representing longitude and latitude data as *x* and *y* variables respectively and then using the borders() function available in the package to add map borders to the plot. The arguments available in this function are as follows:

```
borders(database, regions, fill, color, ...)
```

Here, `database` refers to a part of the preceding map data, and `regions` refers to map regions that can be made available in some map databases. The `fill` and `color` arguments define the colors for filling the inside and borders of the map. The ellipses ... give the possibility of adding additional arguments to the `geom_polygon()` function used to represent the map.

You can see a simple example of the application here; we will first select the US cities with more than `500,000` inhabitants, and then we will add these cities to the US map. Keep in mind that, for this as well as the next examples, you will also need the `maps` package loaded. The following code shows this:

```
require(maps)
```

```
data(us.cities)
big_cities <- subset(us.cities, pop > 500000)
qplot(long, lat, data = big_cities) + borders("state", size = 0.5)
```

In this first example, we used `qplot()` to create the plot to show you the use of this function, but from now on, we will work with `ggplot()`. You can also see how, in this simple example, we used the argument size in the `borders()` function, which is not present in the function arguments listed before since this argument is passed directly to the polygon geometry. As you can see in the plot in *Figure 7.1(A)*, the map represented in this example is the state map, so only state borders are drawn.

The `us.cities` database also contain state information, so we can also select only cities in an individual state. In this next example, we will choose only the cities in `california` and plot them on the `california` map:

```
ca_cities <- subset(us.cities, country.etc == "CA")
ggplot(ca_cities, aes(long, lat)) +
borders(database="county", regions="california", color =
"grey70") + geom_point()
```

As illustrated, in this case, within the `borders()` function, we have selected the `county` map so that the California counties are also represented, and with the `regions` argument, we could select a specific state. You can see the resulting map in *Figure 7.1(B)*:

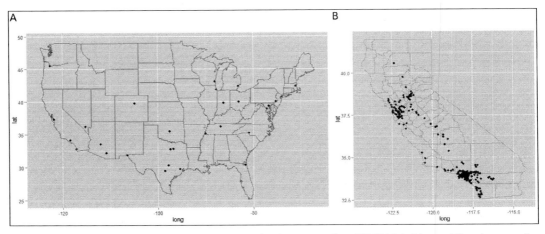

Figure 7.1: Examples of a US state map with cities that have more than 500,000 inhabitants (A) and a map of California counties with all cities available in the database

Until now, we have simply represented the position of the cities, but we can also apply the basic principles of `ggplot2` to these maps, for instance, adding aesthetic mapping to a specific variable. As an example, we will draw the world map with the size of the dot representing the city mapped to the population, which is available in the dataset in the `pop` column. In order to avoid overplotting, we will only plot capital cities, which are identified in the data column `capital`, with `1` indicating that the city is a country's capital. For a description of all data contained in the dataset, you can check the help page with the command `?world.cities`. In this example, we will also change the default colors in the map to give you an idea of what can be modified from the default map appearance:

```
data(world.cities)
capitals <- subset(world.cities, capital == 1)
ggplot(capitals, aes(long, lat)) +
borders("world", fill="lightblue", col="cornflowerblue") +
geom_point(aes(size = pop),col="darkgreen")
```

You can see the resulting plot in *Figure 7.2*.

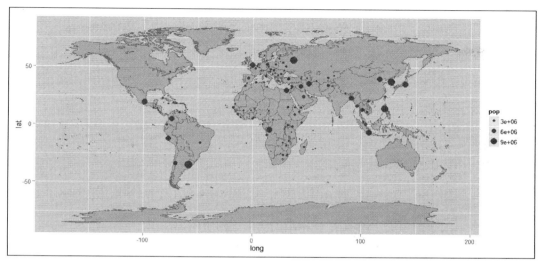

Figure 7.2: A world map with capital cities with points scaled proportional to their population

We can also add text to the map. For instance, we could represent the city's name next to the point indicating the position of each city. For instance, we can represent the cities in `Italy` with a population higher than `500,000` and add their names in the plot. The map of Italy is available in the `maps` package, but there is no dataset containing the Italian cities, so we will use the `world.cities` database and just select the ones in `Italy`:

```
city.Italy <- world.cities[world.cities$country.etc=="Italy",]
city.Italy.big <- subset(city.Italy, pop > 500000)


ggplot(city.Italy.big, aes(long, lat)) + borders("italy") +
geom_point(aes(size = pop)) +
geom_text(aes(long, lat,label=name),hjust=-0.2)
```

Next you can also see a similar example with the world map, where we have included text identifying the country's name next to the capital of the country. In this case, we have only selected cities with a population higher than `5,000,000` to avoid overplotting. The following code shows this:

```
data(world.cities)
capitals <- subset(world.cities, capital == 1)
```

```
capitals.big <- subset(capitals, pop > 5000000)


ggplot(capitals.big, aes(long, lat)) + borders("world") +
geom_point(aes(size = pop)) +
geom_text(aes(long, lat,label=country.etc),hjust=-0.2,size=4)
```

You can see the resulting plots in *Figure 7.3*:

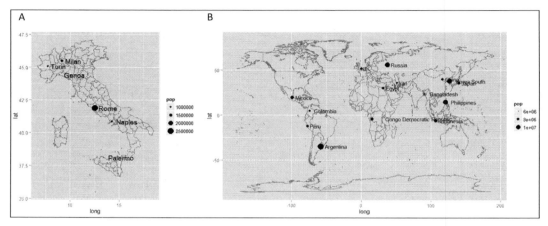

Figure 7.3: A map of Italy with cities with population higher then 500,000 (A)
and a world map with capitals with more than 5,000,000 inhabitants (B)

Finally, when representing cartography data, we can also modify the coordinate systems using the `coord_map()` function available in `ggplot2`. Among the different arguments of this function, one of the most important is the `projection` argument, which defines which map projection to use. These parameters are used by the function `mapproject()` of the `mapproj` package, so you can refer to the help page of this function to know which kinds of projections are available and what they represent.

We will now take the world map we realized previously in *Figure 7.3(B)*, and we will change the coordinate system to spherical coordinates. In this case, we will use the `ortho` projection, which represent a view from infinity. The following code shows this:

```
ggplot(capitals.big, aes(long, lat)) + borders("world") +
geom_point(aes(size = pop)) +
geom_text(aes(long, lat,label=country.etc),hjust=-0.2,size=4) +
coord_map(projection = "ortho", orientation=c(41, 20, 0))
```

We have changed the map orientation by centering the map on Europe. As mentioned earlier, there are many different kinds of projections, so the plot we just made could be alternatively realized using one of the azimuthal projections centered on the North Pole using `coord_map(projection = "azequalarea")` instead. You can see the resulting plots in *Figure 7.4*:

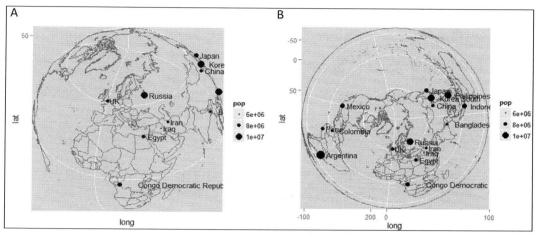

Figure 7.4: A world map with orthographic projection (A) and North Pole-centered projection (B)

Finally, you may also want to add map data that is contained in different databases. In this case, you will need to convert the map data to a data frame and match this data with the other one you want to include on the map. In this way, you will obtain a final dataset containing the map information as well as the additional one you want to represent. To show how it works, we will use one of the datasets provided in the `maps` package that contains the percentage of votes given to the Republican candidate in presidential elections from 1856 to 1976 for the different US states. So, first of all, we will load the datasets and convert the map data to a data frame; in order to do that, we will use the `ggplot2` function `map_data()`:

```
data(votes.repub)

states <- map_data("state")
```

> Be aware that the package `cluster` contains a data frame `votes.repub` with the same data, but in this case, we worked with the data from `maps` to also see how data can be modified and adapted to our needs.

As you can see from running `class(votes.repub)`, this data is provided as a matrix, so first of all, we will need to convert this data to a data frame. Doing so, the column headers will be automatically assigned as dates available in the data, but this may generate issues afterwards since the column headers will be then treated as numeric values. To solve this issue, we will also change the column names, adding `Year` before the date. Moreover, since the names of the US states are reported differently in the two datasets, we will also need to convert the state names to lowercase to make them equal to the one contained in the map data. The following code shows this:

```
repubVotes <- as.data.frame(votes.repub)
names(repubVotes) <- paste("Year",names(repubVotes), sep="")
repubVotes$region <- tolower(rownames(repubVotes))
```

As the last step in our data preparation, we now need to combine the two datasets by matching the state names so that each state will also be associated the corresponding percentage of Republican votes. After using the `match()` function, we will need to reset the column order since this defines the order of the map elements and since this is essential to realize the correct map from the `geom_polygon()` function:

```
finalData <- merge(states, repubVotes, by = "region")
finalData <- finalData[order(finalData$order),]
```

We can now generate our plot, where we will have the US map at the state level with the filling color mapped on the percentage of Republican votes. As illustrated in the final data frame we just created, we have available the percentage of votes for different years, so we will choose the most recent one by selecting the `Year1976` column:

```
ggplot(finalData, aes(long, lat)) +
borders("state") + geom_polygon(aes(group=group,fill=Year1976))
```

You can see the resulting graph in *Figure 7.5*:

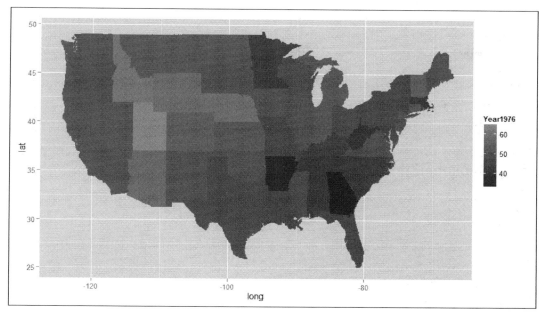

Figure 7.5: A US state map with filling color map on the percentage of Republican votes

Representing maps with ggmap

The ggmap package is a very powerful and versatile tool to extract and reproduce map data using information on static maps from Google Maps, OpenStreetMap, Stamen Maps, or CloudMade Maps. In this context, we will just go through some of the main functionalities, but the authors of this package have provided a very nice and complete description of its use in an article on *The R Journal*; you can find a reference to this article at the end of the chapter.

The basic idea of ggmap is to download a map from a specific database, format it in the context of the layer grammar of ggplot2, and then represent it with an option to add additional ggplot2 elements, such as geometry and statistics. The process is usually divided into two steps—first downloading and formatting the map and then realizing the actual plot. In order to download the maps, you can use the get_map() function, which allows you to specify details of the map, such as the location, zoom, type of map (for instance, terrain, satellite, roadmap, and hybrid), and the Internet service providing the map. As an alternative, you also have specific functions with the general structure get_x, where *x* is replaced by the map provider, so the function get_googlemap() will allow you to download maps from the Google Maps database. Once you have obtained the map and saved it in an R object, you can then recall it and plot it using the ggmap() function. Just as with the qplot() function in ggplot2, in this case too it is the qmap() function that wraps up the two processes and allows you to download and plot the map with one function call. In ggmap, the object positon on the map can be identified by the latitude and longitude coordinates, so if you want to add a red point on a map indicating a specific location, you would need such coordinates. In this respect, the package provides a very helpful function, geocode(), which can provide you with this information. For instance, if you want to know the position coordinates of Eiffel tower, you can simply run the following code:

```
> geocode("Eiffel tower")
```

```
Information from URL: http://maps.googleapis.com/maps/api/geocode/json?ad
dress=Eiffel+tower&sensor=false
```

```
Google Maps API Terms of Service: http://developers.google.com/maps/terms
```

```
          lon          lat
1     2.294481     48.85837
```

As mentioned previously, you can use the qmap() wrapper function to download and represent a map, so in this case too, we can obtain the map of Eiffel tower as shown here:

```
qmap("Eiffel tower", zoom = 14, maptype="terrain")
```

As illustrated, you can use the `zoom` argument to modify the map zoom; this argument can only have integer values from 1 to 21. In *Figure 7.6*, you can see the resulting map, and with this method, the map's appearance is very much different than the one obtained previously with the map package.

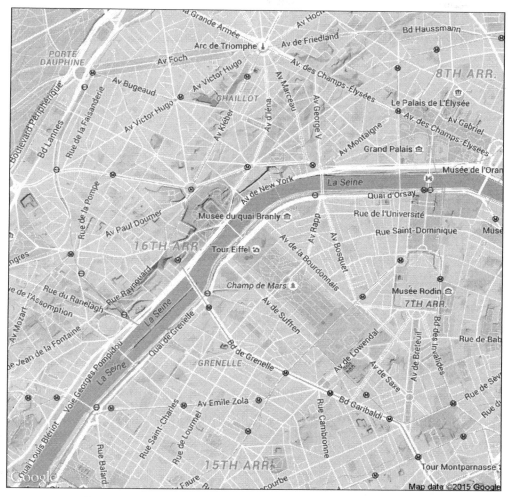

Figure 7.6: A map of the Eiffel tower generated with the ggmap package

This function can also be used with mailing addresses, so the code here will plot a map centered on Google´s headquarters:

```
qmap("1600 Amphitheatre Parkway Mountain View", zoom = 14,
maptype="roadmap")
```

We will now see how to separately download map and then represent it with ggmap(). We will plot the map of Paris and add a marker symbol indicating the position of Eiffel tower:

```
myMarker <- geocode("Eiffel tower")
map <- get_googlemap("Paris", markers = myMarker , scale = 2,zoom
= 12)

ggmap(map, extent = "device")
```

As you can see, in order to represent a marker on the map, we need its coordinates, so we first used the geocode() function to obtain the latitude and longitude of the Eiffel tower, and then we specified in the map that we would like to have the marker corresponding to these coordinates. In this case, we have also used the get_ googlemap() function that searches for a map in Google´s database. Alternatively, we could also have used the get_map() function. The extent argument in the ggmap() function allows you to control how much of the typical ggplot2 plotting format is maintained. You can choose between three different types: normal, where you have the typical ggplot2 axis and layout; panel, where only the axes are maintained; and device, where only the plot area with the map is represented. We will see how the three different options look later on in this section.

On the plot we realize with ggmap, we can also add typical elements from the grammar layer, so, for instance, we can also use datasets from the maps package to add elements on maps downloaded with gmap. Just keep in mind that in order to represent data on maps, you need to have the data of geographic coordinates. So, in this example, we will download the US map, and we will add the position of the different state capitals on top of it as Google Map markers. Next to each capital's location, we will also add its name. The following code shows this:

```
require(maps)
data(us.cities)
### Select only the capitals coordinates
state.capitals <- subset(us.cities, capital == 2)
state.capitals.coord <- state.capitals[,c("long","lat")]
### Download the USA map
mapUSA <- get_googlemap("USA", scale = 2,zoom = 4,
markers=state.capitals.coord)
### Create the ggplot object with the USA map
```

```
USAmap <- ggmap(mapUSA, extent = "device")
### Add the position and names of capital cities
USAmap + geom_text(aes(x = long, y = lat, label=name), data =
state.capitals,hjust=-0.1,size=3.5)
```

As illustrated, we first downloaded the map with the `get_googlemap()` function, and with the `markers` argument, we defined where to add the tracker by providing longitude and latitude data (in this order). In order to do that, we extracted information from `state.capitals` and saved it in a new data frame, `state.capitals.coord`. You may notice how the `grammar` layer elements, such as `geom_text()` in this case, were simply added to a plot element, which we previously created with `ggmap()`. You can see the resulting map in *Figure 7.7*:

Figure 7.7: A US map from Google Maps with markers for US state capitals

In addition to placing markers on the map, we can also connect different points with the argument path in the `get_googlemap()`.function. So, for instance, we can trace the connection between `Eiffel tower` and `Arc de Triomphe` in Paris as shown here:

```
myMarker_Eiffel <- geocode("Eiffel tower")

myMarker_Arc <- geocode("Arc de Triomphe")

myMarkers <- rbind(myMarker_Eiffel,myMarker_Arc)


mapConnections <- get_googlemap("Eiffel tower", scale = 2,zoom = 14,
markers=myMarkers, path=myMarkers)


ggmap(mapConnections, extent = "device")

ggmap(mapConnections, extent = "normal")

ggmap(mapConnections, extent = "panel")
```

As illustrated in the code, we first collected the geographical positions of the two points and then combined these positions in a single dataset, which will then be used to define the marker's position as well as the path to connect. We then created the plot in three different ways using the three options available for the `extent` argument; you can see the three resulting plots in *Figure 7.8 A*, *B*, and *C*:

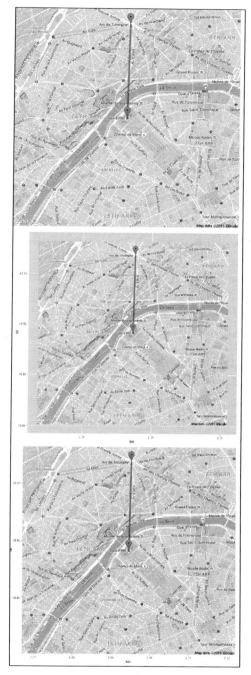

Figure 7.8: Paris maps with connection between the Eiffel Tower and the Arc de Triomphe. The plots are represented as extent = "device" (A), extent = "normal" (B), and extent = "panel" (C)

In the previous example, we connected points on the map directly, without taking into account the actual road connections. The ggmap package also provides a function called route(), which allows you to obtain the route connection between two points.

In the example here, we will again plot the distance between the Eiffel tower and the Arc de Triomphe, but in this case, we will plot the walking route. In order to do that, we will first use the route() function to calculate the distance. This function will also generate the geographical coordinates as well as the distances between the two points, which can, as usual, be provided as a character string. You can see an example of this in the code here:

```
myRoutes <- route("Eiffel tower", "Arc de Triomphe", mode =
"walking", alternatives = TRUE)

myDirections <- get_googlemap("Eiffel tower", scale = 2, zoom = 14,
markers=rbind(myMarker_Eiffel,myMarker_Arc))

ggmap(myDirections, extent = "device") +
geom_leg(aes(x = startLon, y = startLat, xend = endLon, yend =
endLat, col=route), size = 1.5, data = myRoutes)
```

In the function, you can also use the logical argument alternatives if you want Google Maps to provide alternative routes. When this argument is TRUE, the function will provide different alternatives and in the dataset, it will include a column called route, which contains a flag to distinguish between the different route options. In our example, we used this column to assign a different color to the three alternatives. You can see the resulting plot in *Figure 7.9*:

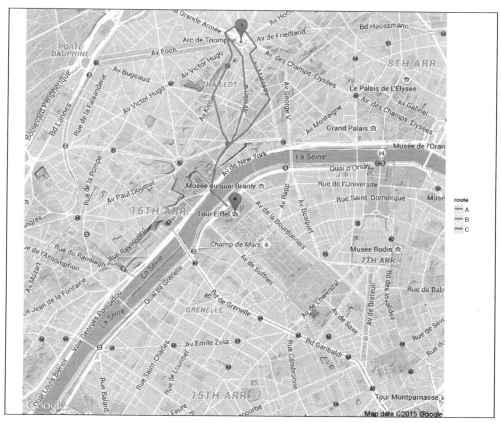

Figure 7.9: A map of Paris with a series of walking routes between the Eiffel Tower and the Arc de Triomphe. Three different route alternatives are showed in different colors

As already mentioned, in this section we have seen simple examples of how map elements and geographical coordinates can be included in `ggplot2` graphics. If you are interested in more complex applications, you can find additional references at the end of the chapter in the *Further reading* section.

Scatterplot matrix with GGally

A scatterplot matrix is a series of scatterplots organized in a grid and often used to describe the relationship between different variables. These plots can range over different degrees of complexity, from merely plotting correlations between variables up to histograms and kernel density plots of distributions that incorporate other variable metadata . If you are already familiar with the `graphics` package, the `pairs()` function can be used to generate a basic scatterplot matrix. Alternatively, the **GGally** package, a helper package of `ggplot2`, can be used to generate scatterplot matrices and other, more complex matrix figures in the `ggplot2` style. It contains templates for different plots to be combined into a plot matrix, a parallel coordinate plot function, as well as a function for making a network plot. The main function available in this package is the `ggpairs()` function, which is able to generate a matrix scatterplot using `ggplot2` graphs,. Its use is quite straightforward. We will see examples with the `iris` dataset, which we have already used previously in the book.

A basic use would simply imply passing the dataset to the function and eventually specifying typical `ggplot2` arguments, such as `color` and `alpha`, in the example here:

```
require(GGally)

ggpairs(iris, color='Species', alpha=0.4)
```

Using the function in this way, it will generate a scatterplot matrix using all columns in the dataset as variables and by selecting the adequate default plot types depending on the nature of the parameter. You can see the plot we obtained in *Figure 7.10*:

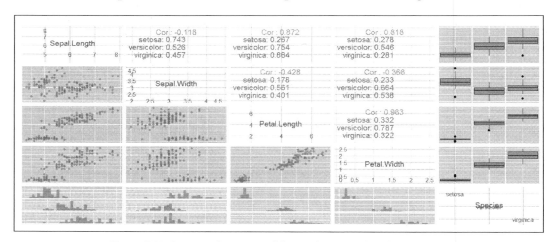

Figure 7.10: A scatterplot matrix of the iris dataset with default settings

As illustrated in the resulting plot, we have represented the data from the three flower species in different colors. The variable names are represented along the diagonals of the matrix and the relationship between variables is described in the various subplots. The plot matrix can be divided into two areas, a lower and an upper part, respectively, below and above the diagonal containing the variables. For continuous variables, such as *Sepal.Length*, *Sepal.Width*, *Petal.Length*, and *Petal.Width*, it represents the correlation between each combination of variables. In the lower part, the data is represented as points, while in the upper part, the data is represented as details of the correlation coefficient. Since we have split the data into groups depending on the values of the `Species` column, this data is spread accordingly. The categorical variable, `Species`, is represented as a histogram in the lower part and as a boxplot in the upper one. A very useful option of the `ggpairs()` function is the possibility of choosing which representation to include in the lower and upper parts of the matrix depending on the type of variable represented. You can use the function arguments `upper` or `lower` and provide a list containing the different plot types. For each parameter combination, only one plot type can be selected. The following is a table summarizing the available plot options depending on the variable combination:

Argument	Variable combination	Plots available
continuous	continuous versus. continuous	`"points"`, `"smooth"`, `"density"`, `"cor"`, `"blank"`
discrete	discrete versus. discrete	`"facetbar"`, `"ratio"`, `"blank"`
combo	continuous versus. discrete	`"box"`, `"dot"`, `"facethist"`, `"facetdensity"`, `"denstrip"`, `"blank"`

The `blank` option is also available and can be used not to represent any plot for that variable combination. So, for instance, if you wanted to have the density plot for the combinations between continuous variables in the upper panels, you would use the following code:

```
ggpairs(iris, upper=list(continuous="density"), color='Species')
```

In the same way, you can also modify the lower plots in a similar way:

```
ggpairs(iris, upper=list(continuous="density"),
lower=list(continuous="smooth"))
```

You can see this last plot in *Figure 7.11*:

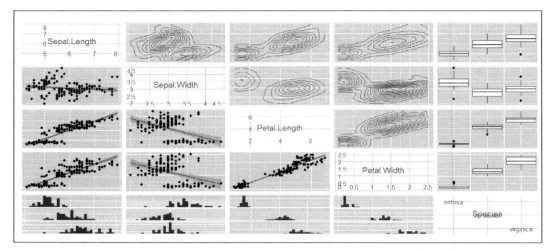

Figure 7.11: A matrix scatterplot or iris dataset with density plots in the upper
area and smooth lines in the lower area for continuous variables

As illustrated in the plot generated, in this case, we have removed the coloring of the
observation depending on the species represented, so, as a consequence, we have
obtained the smooth line in the lower panels as if all the data was coming from the
same source. You can also notice how the panels defining the combination between
the Species variable and all the other variables did not change. These panels, in
fact, fall into the combo category since they are obtained from the combination of
categorical and continuous variables. So, if we also want to modify these panels, for
instance, to have a density plot, and obtain a smooth line for the different flower
species, we can use the following code.

```
ggpairs(iris, upper=list(continuous="density"),
lower=list(continuous="smooth",combo="facetdensity"),
color="Species")
```

You can see the resulting plot in *Figure 7.12*:

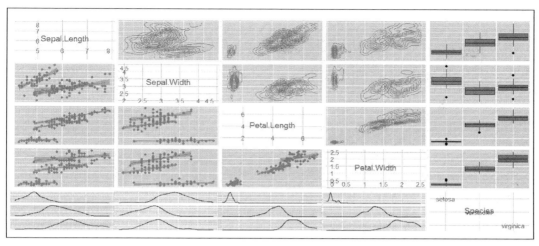

Figure 7.12: A scatterplot matrix of the iris dataset with density plots in the upper area and smooth lines in the lower area for continuous variables and density plots in the lower panels for combo variables

Plotting heatmaps with ggplot2

Heatmaps are representations of matrix data where the individual values contained are represented as colors. Heatmaps can be realized in `ggplot2` using the traditional functions available, but we have also included plots in this chapter that represent very specific type of graphs.

In order to realize a heatmap with `ggplot2`, you will simply need to use the `geom_tile()` function. These plots can be realized usually by representing two variables on both axes and the combinations between these variables are color-mapped using a third variable. Let's first create a simple dataset that we can use.

```
x1 <- seq(-10, 10, length.out = 10)
y1 <- seq(-10, 10, length.out = 10)
d1 <- expand.grid(x = x1, y = y1)


d1$z <- d1$x^2 - d1$y^2
```

We will generate two vectors and then generate all possible combinations between these vectors using the `expand.grid()`.function. We will then just create a third variable, which is a function of the previous ones. What we end up with finally is a 3D curve that can be represented in two dimensions by mapping the third variable to `colors`.

We can use, for instance, the `qplot()` function to easily represent this data as shown here:

```
qplot(x=x, y=y, data=d1, fill=z, geom="tile")
```

As illustrated, we simply had to select the two variables and then map them to a third variable. In the `geom` argument, you can select the `tile` geometry. You can see the resulting picture in *Figure 7.13*:

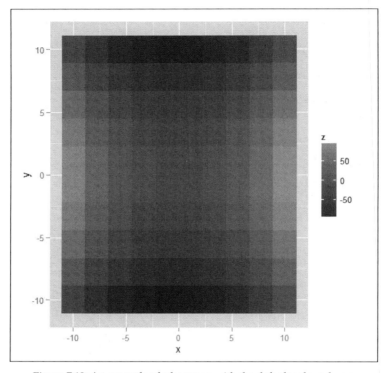

Figure 7.13: An example of a heatmap with the default color scheme

As you can see from the resulting plot, these plots are usually represented as squares obtained by the combinations of the variables represented on the two axes. On the other hand, when the results are particularly dense, the plot can also appear as a continuous shade shifting from one color to the other if you are in a situation where the color mapping variable follows a regular pattern. We will see the same example with a simulation with more data points. Moreover, as an alternative to the default color scheme proposed by `ggplot2`, in these kinds of plots it is particularly effective when representing the values as shades between green and red, as is done in this second example:

```
x2 <- seq(-10, 10, length.out = 100)
```

```
y2 <- seq(-10, 10, length.out = 100)
d2 <- expand.grid(x = x2, y = y2)

d2$z <- d2$x^2 - d2$y^2

ggplot(data=d2, aes(x=x, y=y, fill=z)) +
geom_tile() + scale_fill_gradient(low="red", high="green")
```

In this second example, you have also seen how this plot can be realized with the ggplot() function as an alternative to the use of qplot(). The resulting plot is represented in *Figure 7.14*.

You can find additional examples of this type of plot in the help page of the geom_tile() function, as also reported in the *Further reading* section.

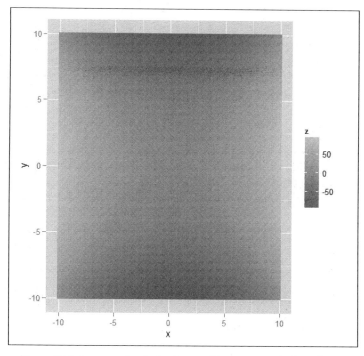

Figure 7.14: An example of a heatmap with a green-red color scheme

Further reading

For maps, refer to the following resources:

- Function `borders()`: `http://docs.ggplot2.org/current/borders.html`
- Function `coord_map()`: `http://docs.ggplot2.org/current/coord_map.html`
- Help page of the function `mapproject()`: `?mapproject`
- Help page of the function `map_data()`: `http://docs.ggplot2.org/current/map_data.html`
- *ggmap: Spatial Visualization with ggplot2, The R Journal Vol. 5/1, D. Kahle and H. Wickham*

For GGally, refer to the following resources:

- Help page of the function `ggpairs()`: `?ggpairs`

For Heatmaps, refer to the following resources:

- Help page of the function `geom_tile()`: `http://docs.ggplot2.org/current/geom_tile.html`

Summary

In this last chapter, we saw the use of `ggplot2` in more specific applications, which, in some cases, may require the use of additional packages. We saw how `ggplot2` can be used to represent geographical data using the `maps` package as well as the more sophisticated `ggmap` package. We then saw how we can realize complex matrix scatterplots with the GGally package and finally how heatmaps can be realized with the `tile` geometry.

Index

A

aesthetic attributes 42, 48, 49
aesthetic mapping
  about 118
  in ggplot2 118-120
  to new stat variables 121-125
axis
  modifying, themes used 159-162
  transformation 147, 148
axis labels
  about 140
  modifying 140, 141
axis scales
  about 143
  axis, transformation 147, 148
  continuous axis 145, 146
  discrete axis 143, 144
  modifying 143
axis tick marks
  removing 148

B

bar charts
  about 53-57, 104
  URL 73
borders() function
  URL 206
box plots (box-and-whisker plots)
  about 59-64, 104
  URL 73
bubble charts
  about 71
  URL 73
bullseye chart 137

C

categorical variables
  and mapping continuous,
    differences 125-127
Comprehensive R Archive Network
  (CRAN) 1
continuous axis
  modifying 145, 146
coord_fixed() function 86
coordinates 42
coordinate system
  about 85-87
  functions 85
coord_map() function
  URL 206
coxcomb diagram 137

D

density plots
  about 49-53, 103
  URL 73
discrete axis
  modifying 143, 144
  order of discrete variables, reversing 144
dot plots 71, 72

E

Eclipse
  about 4
  URL 4
Emacs
  about 5
  URL 5

Emacs Speaks Statistics (ESS)
  about 5
  URL 5

F

facet_grid() function 88
faceting
  about 42, 49, 87
  grid faceting 88-92
  panel orientation, modifying 49
  wrap faceting 94
facets
  used, for adding reference lines 132-134
  used, for adding text 132-134
  using, with themes 165-169
facet_wrap() function 94

G

geom attributes 62
geometric objects 42
geom functions, geometry attributes
  geom_abline 99
  geom_area 99
  geom_bar 99
  geom_blank 99
  geom_boxplot 99
  geom_density 99
  geom_dotplot 99
  geom_errorbar 99
  geom_errorbarh 99
  geom_histogram 99
  geom_hline 99
  geom_jitter 99
  geom_line 99
  geom_path 99
  geom_point 99
  geom_pointrange 99
  geom_ribbon 99
  geom_smooth 99
  geom_text 99
  geom_tile 99
  geom_vline 99
  names, searching 98

geom_tile() function
  URL 206
GGally
  scatterplot matrix with 200-202
ggmap
  used, for plotting maps 183
  used, for representing maps 191-199
ggpairs() function
  URL 206
ggplot2
  about 1
  aesthetic mappings 118-120
  grammar, of graphics 42-44
  layers 95
  packages 2
  references 170
  running 1
  URL 128, 138, 140
  used, for plotting heatmaps 203-205
  used, for plotting maps 183
  used, for representing mapping 184-190
ggplot() function
  and qplot() function, equivalent coding 102
grammar, of graphics 42-44
Graphical User Interface (GUI) 2
graphics package
  about 8
  boxplot, generating 17, 18
  boxplot, generating with
    observations 19, 20
  histogram, generating 21, 22
  histogram, generating with vertical bar on
    median value 23, 24
  implementing 8-10
  scatter plot, generating with line and points
    of one tree 15, 16
  scatter plot, generating with line of
    one tree 13, 14
  scatter plot, generating with points of
    all data 11
graphics tools
  reference link 6
grayscale plots
  creating 140

statistical transformations 42
statistics
  adding 107
stat variables
  aesthetic mapping to 121-124
subset() function 92

T

text
  adding, facets used 132-134
  adding, to plots 128-132
themes
  about 153
  facets, using 165-169

URL 153
  used, for modifying axis 159-162
  used, for modifying legends 154-158
  used, for modifying plot
    background 163, 164
  used, for modifying title 159-162
  using 153, 154
time series 70
Trellis plots 25-27

W

wrap faceting 94

Thank you for buying
ggplot2 Essentials

About Packt Publishing

Packt, pronounced 'packed', published its first book, *Mastering phpMyAdmin for Effective MySQL Management*, in April 2004, and subsequently continued to specialize in publishing highly focused books on specific technologies and solutions.

Our books and publications share the experiences of your fellow IT professionals in adapting and customizing today's systems, applications, and frameworks. Our solution-based books give you the knowledge and power to customize the software and technologies you're using to get the job done. Packt books are more specific and less general than the IT books you have seen in the past. Our unique business model allows us to bring you more focused information, giving you more of what you need to know, and less of what you don't.

Packt is a modern yet unique publishing company that focuses on producing quality, cutting-edge books for communities of developers, administrators, and newbies alike. For more information, please visit our website at www.packtpub.com.

About Packt Open Source

In 2010, Packt launched two new brands, Packt Open Source and Packt Enterprise, in order to continue its focus on specialization. This book is part of the Packt Open Source brand, home to books published on software built around open source licenses, and offering information to anybody from advanced developers to budding web designers. The Open Source brand also runs Packt's Open Source Royalty Scheme, by which Packt gives a royalty to each open source project about whose software a book is sold.

Writing for Packt

We welcome all inquiries from people who are interested in authoring. Book proposals should be sent to author@packtpub.com. If your book idea is still at an early stage and you would like to discuss it first before writing a formal book proposal, then please contact us; one of our commissioning editors will get in touch with you.

We're not just looking for published authors; if you have strong technical skills but no writing experience, our experienced editors can help you develop a writing career, or simply get some additional reward for your expertise.

Building Interactive Graphs with ggplot2 and Shiny [Video]

ISBN: 978-1-78328-433-7   Duration: 01:51 hours

Build stunning graphics and interactive visuals for real-time data analysis and visualization with ggplot2 and Shiny

1. Generate complex interactive web pages using R and produce publication-ready graphics in a principled manner.

2. Use aesthetics effectively to map your data into graphical elements.

3. Customize your graphs according to your specific needs without wasting time on programming issues.

R Graphs Cookbook
Second Edition

ISBN: 978-1-78398-878-5   Paperback: 368 pages

Over 70 recipes for building and customizing publication-quality visualizations of powerful and stunning R graphs

1. Create a wide range of powerful R graphs.

2. Leverage lattice and ggplot2 to create high-quality graphs.

3. Develop well-structured maps for efficient data visualization.

Please check **www.PacktPub.com** for information on our titles

R Graph Essentials

Use R's powerful graphing capabilities to design and create professional-level graphics

David Alexander Lillis

R Graph Essentials

ISBN: 978-1-78355-455-3   Paperback: 190 pages

Use R's powerful graphing capabilities to design and create professional-level graphics

1. Learn how to use Base R to analyze your data and generate statistical graphs.

2. Create attractive graphics using advanced functions such as qplot and ggplot for research and analysis.

3. A step-by-step guide, packed with examples using real-world data sets that can prove helpful to R programmers.

R Data Analysis Cookbook

Over 80 recipes to help you breeze through your data analysis projects using R

Viswa Viswanathan   Shanthi Viswanathan

R Data Analysis Cookbook

ISBN: 978-1-78398-906-5   Paperback: 342 pages

Over 80 recipes to help you breeze through your data analysis projects using R

1. Analyse data with ready-to-use and customizable recipes.

2. Discover convenient functions to speed-up your work and data files.

3. Demystifies several R packages that seasoned data analysts regularly use.

Made in the USA
Lexington, KY
19 August 2019